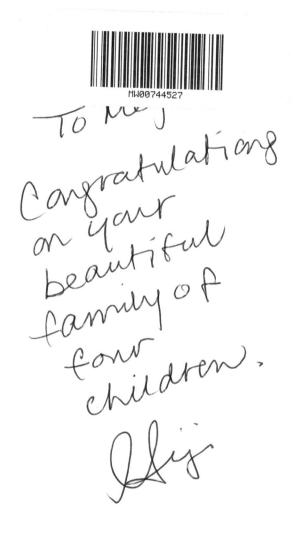

To M...

Congratulations on your beautiful family of four children.

Liz

THE Motherhood CLUB™
Making a Difference One Kiss at a Time

How to Discipline Your Child with Love and Patience

There's a
Perfect Little Angel
in Every *Child*

Gigi Schweikert

HOWARD
PUBLISHING CO.

OUR PURPOSE AT HOWARD PUBLISHING IS TO:

- *Increase faith* in the hearts of growing Christians
- *Inspire holiness* in the lives of believers
- *Instill hope* in the hearts of struggling people everywhere
  BECAUSE HE'S COMING AGAIN!

There's a Perfect Little Angel in Every Child © 2005 by Gigi Schweikert
All rights reserved. Printed in the United States of America
Published by Howard Publishing Co., Inc.
3117 North 7th Street, West Monroe, Louisiana 71291-2227
www.howardpublishing.com

05 06 07 08 09 10 11 12 13 14   10 9 8 7 6 5 4 3 2 1

Edited by Michele Buckingham
Interior design by John Mark Luke Designs

Library of Congress Cataloging-in-Publication Data

Schweikert, Gigi, 1962–
    There's a perfect little angel in every child : guiding your children to a bright future / Gigi Schweikert.
        p. cm.
    Includes bibliographical references.
    ISBN 1-58229-415-1
    1. Child rearing—Religious aspects—Christianity. 2. Parenting—Religious
aspects—Christianity. 3. Mother and child—Religious aspects—Christianity. I. Title.

BV4529.S39 2005
248.8'45—dc22

2004054329

Contents

To my own
Little Angels—

Ashley, Genevieve,
Marielle, and William

Acknowledgments

"Are you finished yet?" came the frequent calls of my children during the writing of this book. One thing I discovered: writing about children is much easier than actually caring for them. At times the daily discipline struggles in my own home made me doubt that there were *any* ideas that could make parenting easier, much less my own. But what I realized and what I know is that there's no perfect way to raise children. You love them and lead them, and then you let them fly.

I want to thank my children for their patience and support. Thanks, too, to my husband, Al, for his complete love and dedication to our family, and for stepping in as "Mom" when I was busy writing. And thanks to my own parents, who have always given me total and unconditional love.

Jim Greenman encouraged me to write my first parenting article when I was a new mom, and he has been my writing mentor and friend ever since.

The faith of Margie Negri and her determination to reread everything I wrote, while caring for her own three children, helped shape this book.

Denny and Philis Boultinghouse of Howard Publishing have a passion for books and, more importantly, for the people behind them.

Editor Michele Buckingham made my manuscript a book. She is full of ideas and enthusiasm.

Kathy Fiegley and her staff at Kangaroo Kids remind me every day of the patience and energy it takes to really love and care for children.

Special thanks to my grown-up mommy girlfriends who keep me laughing: Renee Fusco, my dreamer; Margie Negri, my believer; Basha Nelson, my artist; Lina Schmidt, my determination; and Kris Urmston, my realist.

And thank you, God, for all the perfect little angels!

I'm a *Mother* and I'm Ok—I *Think*

Every night after I scrub four kids (and sometimes the dog), read just one more story, give four extra kisses, fall into bed, and recognize that the man next to me is my husband (I usually only see him as I whiz by, so he looks different when he's not blurry), I close my eyes and ask myself, "Was I a good mother today?" And a little voice inside of me says, "What do you think?"

To be honest, I'm not always sure. If exhaustion has any direct correlation to good parenting, then I'm at the top of the class most days.

Actually, if moms were to receive a report card each quarter, I think mine would read:

Full of Love . . . . A

Prone to Crankiness C

1

Good Cook . . . . C-

Organized . . . . Incomplete

Willing to Learn . . . . A

Am I a good mother? I know that when I relax and stop comparing myself to others, I feel more confident about my role. I'm not perfect, by any means. I'm not always the best mom I can be. But I'm always trying—and that's got to count for something.

In the pages that follow, I want to share with you some of the lessons I've learned about being a mom. And the first lesson is this: in every child, there is a perfect little angel. As moms it's our job to draw these perfect little angels out—to teach them how to be who they really are. It's our job to teach them how to fly.

I've discovered that we don't have to be perfect moms to do this. We just have to love our children unconditionally and be willing to learn. We just have to try.

The next time you look at your child, tell yourself, "There are wings in there somewhere." Your perfect little angel is meant to soar! You just have to get those wings to start flapping.

How can you guide your child toward a bright future?

Teaching
Your Angel
How to *Fly*

There's a perfect little angel in every child. I know that's hard to believe—especially when it's *your* child who is continually testing the limits (and your patience). It's your child who has thrown himself on the floor in the grocery aisle and created a shopping-cart traffic jam, all because you won't buy him frozen pizzas shaped like jungle animals. It's your child who rolls her eyes and refuses a simple request, adamantly claiming, "You're ruining my life." It's your child who says, "I hate you. Go away. I don't want to go home," just because you happen to be the one picking him up from preschool. Children know just how loud to say mean things so that all the other adults within shouting distance hear, making you feel like the worst mother in the world.

You're not.

You're just the mother of a perfect little angel.

Stepping Up to the Halo

When you hear the words "perfect little angel," what kind of child do you picture? One who is adorably dressed, compliant and tame, with impeccable manners, cooperative, reasonable, easy to please? I suppose some children can step up to that halo; but frankly, they're few and far between.

For most of us, discovering the perfect little angel in our children takes a little digging beneath the surface. It takes knowing what to *really* look for.

What does a perfect little angel look like?

Perfect little angels rarely sport a halo, wings, or even clean clothes. They often wear green plastic froggy boots so they can splash in mud puddles and scoop tadpoles out of the creek. You can identify perfect little angels by looking at their hands: they're dirty from coloring-book marathons, earthworm digs, and forays into Mommy's makeup drawer. You may even find traces of white paste under their nails, evidence of their determined effort to peel off all the wallpaper in the bathroom.

Perfect little angels forget to do their homework, leave the kitchen cabinets wide open, and never wipe the cookie crumbs off the counter. They need to be reminded to put their dirty clothes in the hamper, say their prayers, and brush their teeth. When you call perfect little angels, they don't come, because a car trip to run errands with Mommy interferes with their resolve to collect all the pillows and cushions in the house and stack them into a huge pile suitable for diving. Appearing to wander aimlessly at times, perfect little angels smear fingerprints on newly washed windows and dump baskets full of anything for the sheer pleasure of seeing the contents emptied onto the floor. And even though they can't seem to remember what Mommy asked them to do two minutes ago, they spend long hours concentrating on burying every block they own, large and small, in the potted plants.

You're not going to discover your perfect little angel by looking with a critical eye for perfect manners, perfect behavior, or a perfect wardrobe. No, you'll only find the perfect little angel in your child by looking through eyes of wonder and love for limitless energy, creativity, and even testing.

You see, perfect little angels are very busy trying to make sense of the world around them. They learn by exploring, experimenting, and testing the limits of their environment— and their mothers. They especially like to test us when we're tired, in a hurry, or around people we want to impress. Perfect little angels will eventually be responsible, independent, and capable individuals. But for now, we have to remember: they're just children.

When you are angry with your perfect little angel and don't feel particularly loving and accepting, stop for a moment and think about how cute he is when he's asleep.

What can you expect from your angel?

On the way to earning their wings and halo, perfect little angels almost certainly will:

- Use their curiosity to explore and learn about the world around them (This includes putting things in their noses.)

- Display their individuality through unique interests, temperaments, and moods (These moods can change daily, so predicting what's in store at any particular time can be next to impossible.)

- Become social beings while maintaining their uniqueness

- Differ in how they learn and the type of care they need

- Develop at their own pace and in their own way

- Let others know their feelings, needs, and wants—often using dramatic and inappropriate methods (Sometimes a tantrum is the only thing they can think of.)

- Expect the unconditional love and acceptance of the adults who care for them

- Test all limits by using their actions to check the reactions of people and things (Sometimes they drive you crazy because that's how they get your attention—and because it's fun!)

- Use their bodies to test the physical properties of people, things, and space (Smashing into another group of toddlers is a great way to say, "I'm here.")

- Explode with energy (They love to run and scream in wide-open spaces like the airport, the mall, and the grocery store, and especially those places where people are supposed to be quiet.)

- Explode with frustration because they have little patience (Let's admit it, we mothers don't always have much patience either.)

- Be contrary by refusing, defying, and resisting others, because they are learning that they can exert control (They know that adults have ultimate control, of course. Case in point: We can eat cookies whenever we want. They can't.)

- Be cooperative

- Be responsible

- Act silly

- Experience intense separation anxiety at times (Perfect little angels love everything about their mommies, and they feel safest and happiest when they're with them. That's true not only for babies and toddlers, but for older angels too. All children want and need time with Mom.)

- Develop self-confidence

- Look to others to recognize and appreciate the wonderful person that each of them is and will become

Getting Those Wings to Fly

Yes, there is a perfect little angel in every child. Sometimes we even see the angel (usually when we're at home or in the car, when nobody else is around to witness it and praise our mothering skills). All children have positive angel moments. The question is, how can we get the angel traits to show up on a more regular basis? How can we get those wings to fly?

The answer is a word that may surprise you: discipline.

What is discipline?

Discipline is teaching our children how to act in a socially acceptable way, how to acknowledge their emotions but control their reactions, and how to understand the way the world works and find their place in it. It's firmly but lovingly guiding our children, having hope for our children, developing self-esteem in the little ones and even the big ones, and uncovering the perfect little angel within. This discovery process sometimes takes an extra measure of mommy patience and mommy persistence. Every child is different. But every child is worth the effort and the love we must commit to the process.

Through discipline we teach our children to develop good

behaviors instead of inappropriate ones. We help them understand the difference between right and wrong. We teach them to make positive choices instead of negative ones. The result is that when they're all grown up and we're no longer there to guide them, they'll still know the right thing to do.

For some reason, we often associate discipline with punishment. Certainly, there ought to be logical consequences for every action. But effective discipline actually uses punishment sparingly. We're much more likely to help our children learn and succeed if we think about discipline as a teachable moment, not necessarily a punishable one.

Think about discipline as a teachable moment
and not necessarily a punishable one.

Our society often complains about the lack of respect and responsibility in children these days. At the same time, mothers overindulge their children, feel guilty about setting limits, lack consistency, and resist holding their children accountable for their actions. We need to understand: Discipline is not negative; it's not mean; it's not punishment. Rather, discipline is everything we do, say, and teach our children in order to grow them up to be wise, caring, and socially responsible adults. Discipline is, quite simply, raising our kids.

What dreams do you have for your angel?

We all have great dreams for our children—although I have to admit, sometimes my dream only extends to bedtime, when they're all asleep and I can finally sit down and relax for a few minutes. But when I'm not wishing away the day, I dream of my children's futures: happy futures filled with family and fortune, love and laughter, acceptance and happiness.

What do you want for your child's future? Try to envision that jelly-faced, sticky-handed toddler—the one who just figured out how to knock all the pictures off the wall in the hallway with a broomstick—as an adult. What does he look like? Sometimes all I can imagine is that same toddler in an oversized shirt and pants, wearing Daddy's shoes, still sporting a jelly smile. It's hard to imagine my son all grown up! And yet I know that every time I remind him to say thank you, every time I send him to his room for calling his sister a "stupid-head," and every time I teach him to give to others who are less fortunate, I'm shaping the adult he will one day be.

I have to love him enough now to correct him when he is out of bounds and put him on the right path, because it will only get harder later. A toddler's defiant no's left unchecked lead to a teenager's less correctable no's and worse. If you hit your sister when you're a preschooler, you go to your room. If you hit anyone when you're older, you go to jail! And unfortunately, our jails are filled with hundreds and even thousands of angels who were never taught to fly.

What do you want your child to be when she's all grown up? Consider the following list of possible characteristics, and check the ones that seem especially important to you:

___ Financially secure

___ Well-educated

___ Honest

___ Well-adjusted

___ Polite

___ Patient

___ Happy

___ Content

___ Civic minded

___ Generous

___ God centered

___ Adventurous

___ Friendly

___ Empathetic

___ Kind

Did you check them all? I think most moms want their children to be all of these things and more. Now go back to the list and select your top five. That's harder to do! Next, take the five you picked and rank them in order of importance. What is the single most important characteristic that you want to see developed in your perfect little angel? The characteristics we value and want most for our children will shape the way we discipline them and how we set our priorities as mothers.

The characteristics you value and want most for
your child will shape the way you discipline her.

We may think that if our children aren't always polite, it's no big deal—until we realize that the opposite of polite is rude. Who wants to be responsible for having raised a rude adult? Most of us would rather spend time imagining what we want our children to be instead of what we *don't* want them to be. Still, it's worth looking at some of the not-so-positive characteristics that we can build into our children if we're not careful. Take a moment to consider the following list. For me, reading this list is a real motivator for being more patient, persistent, and proactive in my parenting.

- Poor, instead of financially secure

- Illiterate, instead of well-educated

- Deceitful, instead of honest

- Dysfunctional, instead of well-adjusted

- Rude, instead of polite

- Intolerant, instead of patient

- Miserable, instead of happy

- Disgruntled and restless, instead of content

- Self-serving, instead of civic minded

- Stingy, instead of generous

- Godless or ambivalent, instead of God centered

- Fearful, instead of adventurous

- Reclusive, instead of friendly

- Uncaring, instead of empathetic

- Mean, instead of kind

Is your child likely to fall to one or the other extreme?

Of course, in each of these categories, there is a continuum. All of us, parents and children, fall within different ranges at certain times in our lives and even from day to day. We will not all be as financially secure as we might wish to be; neither will our children. We probably have different definitions of what "financial security" means anyway! But I'm sure that as mothers we want our children to have jobs, homes, food, and families of their own someday. And whether or not our kids have lots of money to give away, we want them to be generous and gracious toward others, not self-centered and stingy.

Every child is different. But all children can be guided through loving discipline to develop—along with their own unique personalities, skills, talents, and interests—behavior that is positive, socially acceptable, and responsible. All children can be taught that being a good person is the first step to being a successful person.

How can you help your child succeed?

Avoiding
Angel Grabbers
and
Success Zappers

Sometimes we busy moms overlook or ignore the simple steps of parenting. We let routines slip, dinners slide, and give in to whining and pleading much too often. We stop at just one more store, make just one more phone call, or chat just a little longer with a friend, disregarding that little voice inside our heads that says, "You really should be attending to your children." Later we wonder why our perfect little angels can't seem to behave the way we want them to. We have to stop and ask ourselves, "Are we setting our children up to succeed? Or are we putting them in situations that guarantee failure?"

The probability that our children will behave well greatly increases when we meet their physical needs and provide structure in their lives. Yet we often overlook these keys in the busyness of modern parenting. Children (like adults) need proper sleep, nutritious meals, predictable routines, clear rules and limitations, and day-to-day consistency. The absence of any of these necessary ingredients is a real angel grabber and success zapper:

The probability that your child will behave well
greatly increases when you meet her physical
needs and provide structure in her life.

Think about it. Isn't it true that children misbehave most often when they're tired, hungry, or expected to sit for long periods of time? Don't they get into the most trouble when they don't know what to expect or what's expected of them? As moms we can help our perfect little angels succeed by learning how to avoid these five angel grabbers and success zappers. Let's look more closely at each one.

Success Zapper #1:
Lack of Sleep

One of the most common reasons perfect little angels misbehave or lose control is lack of sleep. You hear it all the time: "He's tired." "She needs a nap." Sleep deprivation makes children cranky, easily frustrated, and lowers their level of tolerance.

If you have an angel who is frequently out of control, the first thing you should do is document his sleep patterns. Over the next week, write down how much time your child actually sleeps during naps and at night. Omit the time he may be resting quietly in his crib or bed.

How much sleep does your angel need?

The American Academy of Pediatrics recommends that children consistently get at least nine to eleven hours of sleep each night.[1] Children who are sleep deprived, even slightly, are more likely to have health problems as well as behavior problems. Talk to your pediatrician about the length of night sleep and naps appropriate for your angel, and then establish a reasonable bedtime routine for him. Once he begins to enjoy appropriate sleep, you'll see an almost immediate change in his behavior.

Angel **Tip**

One of the major reasons children misbehave is lack of sleep.
Make sure your child is getting nine to eleven hours
of sleep each night. (Infants require even more sleep.
Speak to your child's pediatrician about the amount
of sleep necessary for your child.)

Perhaps you're thinking, "But you don't understand. Just getting my perfect little angel to sleep on time is a major discipline problem." You're not alone. For most of us, bedtime isn't anything like what we see on television: freshly bathed children in soft flannel pajamas who brush their teeth, listen to a story, say their prayers, whisper "I love you, Mommy," and then fall right to sleep.

In the real world, getting children to stay in their beds until morning can be a real battle. But it's a battle worth fighting and winning—for their sakes and for ours. Adequate sleep is essential for our children's healthy growth. With regular rest, they will learn more easily and behave better. And after they're tucked snuggly into bed, we will have some greatly deserved time to spend alone or with our husbands, getting the refreshment *we* need. Establishing a healthy sleep routine for our perfect little angels helps us regain and maintain our motherhood sanity!

How can you establish a bedtime routine?

Here are some tips for starting a new bedtime routine. Keep in mind that making a bedtime change in your child's life will require consistent implementation on your part over a period of weeks. But stick with it!

- Develop a consistent, relaxing "before" bedtime routine with your child. Do the same things every night in the same order. These may include a bath, reading a book, listening to a tape, or having a short conversation with her about her day.

- Set and stick to a regular bedtime. If your child is in elementary school, he could be allowed to read before going to sleep, but he must stay in his room. Tell him, "You don't have to sleep, but you do have to stay in your bed."

- Avoid giving your child any foods or beverages containing caffeine or any liquids at all two hours before bedtime.

- Make your child's bedroom comfortable. A cool, quiet room with low lighting is most conducive for sleep.

Although lack of sleep may be one of the reasons children misbehave, it's not an excuse. "She called me a name, so I had to hit her." "I wanted to play with that toy, so I had to take it." A perfect little angel may be tired, but that doesn't make bad behavior OK! Children, like adults, must be held accountable for their actions. We can help them out by making sure they get a good night's sleep—and that we do too.

Success Zapper #2:
Skipping Meals and Poor Nutrition

Nutrition's effect on children's behavior has long been a debated topic among researchers. But ask any veteran mom, and I guarantee she'll tell you that children are susceptible to the "birthday buzz," a kiddy high, induced by an overload of sugary treats. Some experts argue that it's just the excitement of the event, not the food, that causes the behavioral change. But more and more, medical research is catching up with moms. Studies are beginning to show that nutrition may even play a role in such behaviors as Attention Deficit Hyperactivity Disorder (ADHD) and autism.

When it comes to your child, remember: you're the expert. You don't need statistical data to back you up. If you notice that your child's behavior regularly changes for the worse whenever she consumes certain foods, consult your pediatrician. You may want to eliminate or reduce the amount of those foods in her diet.

They're usually the stuff that needs to be eliminated, anyway, like soda, caffeine, artificial colors, excessive sugar, and fatty foods. Do keep in mind, however, that children have different nutritional needs than adults. A certain amount of fat is necessary for growth and proper brain development. Don't change your child's diet without medical assistance.

What if your child skips meals?

Healthy, well-proportioned meals, including breakfast, feed not only the body but also the mind. Several scientific studies have found that hunger—even the temporary hunger of skipping one meal—can affect children's attention span, behavior, ability to concentrate, and cognitive performance. The American School Food Service Association, for example, found that fourth-grade students who had the least protein intake in their diets also had the lowest achievement scores on standardized tests.[2]

Don't let your child skip meals.
Hunger can affect his attention span, behavior,
ability to concentrate, and cognitive performance.

Ever been on a diet for quick weight loss? At some point, you think that you just might gnaw off your own arm if you don't get some food! You get a headache; you're less tolerant; in fact,

20

you're downright cranky. Well, if that's how you react to food deprivation, imagine how hunger adversely affects your child's behavior—that perfect little angel who's only beginning to learn how to control her emotions and reactions. The obvious way to avoid this angel-grabber is to offer her healthy meals and snacks on a consistent basis.

Should you force your child to eat?

Some children need more encouragement to stay focused on eating than others, but all children will eat when they are hungry. We shouldn't force them to eat or use food as a bribe. The issue, after all, is nutrition, not control. If you're having trouble getting your child to sit still for big meals, try offering minimeals throughout the day. Snacks-to-go are OK for emergencies. But don't offer your child food every time you want him to settle down. Not only is that not a good discipline strategy, it can lead to overeating and emotional eating (using food as a comfort tool), possibly bringing on childhood obesity and other related childhood illnesses.

Success Zapper #3:
No Routine

When you go to the movies or to church, do you find yourself sitting in the same row every time? Do you need a shower or cup of coffee in the morning before you can get started?

Imagine going to the grocery store and finding that the stock clerks had moved all the food to different aisles overnight. Every night they move the food again, so that no matter how many times you go to that store, you never know where to find anything. How would you feel?

We humans are creatures of habit. We prefer routine. When we know what to expect, we feel secure, comfortable, trusting, and less anxious. That's exponentially true for children.

Why is a routine important for your child?

If you have a child in preschool, you probably share my amazement at the way all the children rest or take a nap at the same time each school day. When those same children are at home, we can barely get them to sit down, much less close their eyes! What accounts for the difference? Many factors are involved, but the main ones are that the school has clear expectations, consistently enforced rules, and, as most teachers will tell you, routine. Children in a school setting have the same routine every day.

Even into early elementary school, children don't have the same sense of time that adults do. They ask questions like "How long is an hour?" and "Is today my birthday party?" And we answer, "An hour is as long as two Barney shows," or "Your party is in two days, after pizza day at school." But children do have a sense of sequence, the order of the day, cause and effect, and what comes next. Even an infant understands, *When I cry, someone comes.* A toddler learns, *I can't go outside until I put on my coat.*

And a preschooler knows, *After my bath comes a bedtime story.* These are routines they have come to depend on.

How will a routine help your child?

A routine gives children a structured environment that helps to reduce anticipatory anxiety (the anxiety that comes from not knowing what to expect) and fosters feelings of security, comfort, and trust. When children know what to expect, they feel more in control and therefore behave better and learn more easily. Through routine they develop a better understanding of their world and how they are supposed to function in it.

If your child knows what to expect next,
she's more likely to behave appropriately.

Sometimes we don't realize the positive impact that routine has in our children's lives until there is the absence of routine. Think, for example, about the struggles that children commonly go through after such drastic changes as a move, the birth of a sibling, or divorce. But even more subtle deviations from everyday routine can affect our children's behavior. Holiday celebrations are a perfect example. Although holidays provide an exciting and welcome change from the norm, perfect little angels are more likely to act out during holiday festivities (when we want them to be on their best behavior in front of all the relatives).

Shouldn't you teach your child to be flexible?

Sure, children should learn to be flexible and adapt to change. But that doesn't mean they shouldn't stick to a regular schedule. They have plenty of opportunities to experience change and exercise flexibility within the structure of their daily routine. Remember, they're only at the beginning of the learning curve. They're still trying to figure out how to settle their bodies down for sleep and how to react when someone comes over to play. Perfect little angels get excited about a friend coming over for a play date until it dawns on them that this new kid is going to play with all of their toys. Surprise! Time for a lesson in flexibility!

Most of us have had the experience of going away on a great vacation—one that was lots of fun and a great change of pace—only to return home eager to fall back into our daily routine. Human beings prefer to live with some sense of routine. Young children crave routine and the security of seeing familiar people and surroundings every day. They can handle change and learn flexibility best within the comfortable pattern of daily life.

Success Zapper #4: Absence of Clear Rules and Limitations

As mothers we have lots of expectations about the behavior "destination" we want our children to reach, but we often forget to give them the "road map"—the clear, specific rules of acceptable behavior they need to stay on course. It sounds silly, but we often don't tell our children the rules we expect them to live by!

Why are rules important for your child?

Think about life without rules. The thought of driving over the speed limit down the main thoroughfare (mothers are usually running late) or taking as many outfits as you can carry from the mall without paying may seem momentarily pleasurable. But we all know the chaos that would ensue in the absence of rules and limitations. Socialized life depends upon a framework of rules and the self-discipline of individuals to respect those guidelines of behavior.

For children, rules provide safety, security, and reasonable limits that teach them how to live life successfully. For example, let's say we make a rule: "When we go to the store, we buy only the things that are on Mommy's list. You cannot beg Mommy to buy something else that you happen to see." Of course, it's natural for us to want to give our children things we didn't have when we were growing up. And in a world of "more is better," it's easy to confuse what children *want* with what they actually *need*. Often we respond to every "I want" because we can, and not necessarily because we should. How many pairs of expensive sneakers does one child need? Should a child expect to get something every time you go to a store?

Without clear rules and limitations, our children will not be able to learn patience and self-control (that is, you can't always have what you want when you want it). They will never experience the self-satisfaction of working toward and attaining a goal, such as buying their own expensive sneakers. But if we teach them to comply with our simple mommy rules today, they'll be prepared to follow the more complex rules and laws of society tomorrow.

By teaching your child to comply with simple rules today, you prepare him to follow the more complex rules and laws of society tomorrow.

How do you set rules for your child?

We'll talk more about setting appropriate expectations for your child in chapter 3. But here are some general guidelines for preparing a road map of rules for your child.

- *Limit the number of rules.* Establish a few simple rules for your very young child, and increase the number and complexity of rules as he grows.

- *Phrase the rules in the positive when possible.* Tell your child "Please walk," instead of "No running."

- *Make your rules specific.* "Brush your teeth before you listen to the bedtime story."

- *Remind your child of the rules frequently.* Help her succeed. "You must stay in your seat in the restaurant." "Remember to say thank you after the party."

- *Ask your child to help you decide the rules.* "There are toys on the floor, and people could fall on them. What should we

26

do?" "I want to know where you are at all times. How can we make sure that happens?"

- *Be willing to change the rules*—but avoid saying, "No, no, no, yes." Changing the rules and giving in to your child's persistent pleading are different. "I think you're old enough to stay up later now."

- *Expect your child to break the rules.* Some angels will continually try to bend the rules. But even the most perfect angel will have an off day. Approach every broken rule as an opportunity to teach and guide.

- *Follow through.* Establishing the rules is the easy part. The hard part is finding the energy and determination to follow through, to be tough enough to say, "We're not buying anything at the store except groceries. Please don't ask." "You can't watch that television program." "It's time to turn off the computer and go outside and play." It's so much easier to give in and let our children do what they want. Perfect little angels can be so persistent, and mothers can be so tired! But for our children's sakes, we have to dig deep and find the courage and stamina we need to stand firm.

Success Zapper #5:
Inconsistency

Many of us don't follow through with consistent discipline for any number of reasons. Maybe we feel guilty that we haven't spent a lot of time with our children, and we think that buying them something at the store when they whine for it or letting them stay up late because they don't want to go to bed will make up for our lack of attention. The problem is, our kids may feel happier and we may feel less guilty for the moment, but the pleasure is only temporary. We pay a hefty price the next time a discipline issue arises, and our children are confused by our inconsistency.

Without getting into a debate over which is more important, quantity time or quality time (angels need both!), I will say this: children need us to be parents, not friends. Just as they find security in routine, they find security in parents who set limits and consistently enforce them. That's not to say we should all become overbearing, I'm-watching-every-move-you-make moms, waiting for our children to step out of line so we can be right there to punish them. Rather, we need to be I'm-with-you-every-step-of-the-way moms who consistently nudge our angels back in line, reminding them there are consequences for the choices they make.

Take a look at the following list of reasons moms fail to discipline their angels, and check the ones that apply to you most often:

___ Guilt

___ Exhaustion

___ Frustration (giving up or giving in)

___ Embarrassment in front of others

___ Focusing on other things

___ Lack of effective strategies for discipline

___ High level of tolerance for noise and movement

___ Desire to avoid conflict

___ Lack of time

___ False thinking that says, "I shouldn't discipline my child until she's older."

How many did you check? Whatever reasons we have for failing to discipline, we must find ways to change our thinking, our schedules, or both.

Be consistent in your discipline.
Your child needs your guidance.

Shouldn't you wait until your child is older to really discipline her?

Some moms think they should hold off discipline until their toddlers and preschoolers are older, when they are better able to understand the reasons for good behavior. But that's like waiting to train a puppy until he's a dog. Why wait and clean up really big messes later, when you can begin guiding your child now and avoid the messes altogether (or at least deal with smaller ones)?

Our expectations have to be realistic and developmentally appropriate. And it's true that children may develop and understand concepts such as compassion better when they are older. But that doesn't mean they shouldn't be taught not to hit someone else, even if they don't understand how much hitting can physically and emotionally hurt the other person.

Does disciplining a two-year-old for hitting her brother sound harsh? Not at all! Remember, when we think of discipline as a teachable moment and not necessarily a punishable one, we're more likely to help our children succeed. As we've said, effective discipline rarely uses punishment, although there *are* logical consequences for every action. Discipline is socialization and guidance. It's teaching our children how to act in the world and react to others. Why wait until they are older?

What does inconsistency teach your child?

As moms, our inconsistency becomes our children's consistency. Think about it: children learn to work and play in ways that help them get what they want. For those children whose basic physical and emotional needs aren't being met, this may be a necessary survival technique. For all children, it's how they influence their world—including us. Children are just waiting for us to give up or give in, and once they see how to accomplish that, they'll use that skill over and over again. If a tantrum in the store gets an angel the candy he wants, he'll try a tantrum again. If touching her new baby sister gets an angel the attention from Mommy that she wants, she'll touch the baby again. If making a scene in front of Mommy's friends makes Mommy give in to one more video game, then a perfect little angel will be sure to use that tactic the next time.

*Once your child learns what it takes to get you to
give up or give in, he will use that skill again and
again to obtain what he wants. Be strong!*

Children understand cause and effect. If we are inconsistent in certain situations, regardless of our good intentions, they will learn that their inappropriate behavior is the way they can get what they want. The bottom line is that perfect little angels can be taught to act the way *we* want them to or the way *they* want to. Our consistency or inconsistency is what makes the difference.

Of course, no mother is perfect. Maybe you lost track of time one day and stayed on the phone with your best friend when you should have been putting your child down for a nap. Maybe you finished a project later than you expected, and you had to get dinner at the less-than-healthy drive-through. Maybe you were especially tired one afternoon and gave in to a persistent whine in the checkout line. Don't despair! Every angel is going to get grabbed or zapped on occasion. But the more we understand about the impact of angel grabbers and success zappers on our children, the more vigilant we will want to be. Ultimately, our children's success depends upon it.

How can you set realistic expectations?

Showing
Your Angel
Where to *Stand*

When a baseball player is up to bat, he knows to stand over the plate. A basketball player knows to shoot a foul shot from the foul line. A golfer knows to tee up between the two markers. Every game has rules, and the better you know the rules, the more likely you are to succeed.

Children are eager to learn the rules of life, and it's our responsibility as parents to teach them. Of course, it's much more fun to teach them to play baseball than responsibility or respect. The rules of life seem so much more complicated than the rules of baseball, and they are. But that's what being a mother is all about: guiding our perfect little angels to understand the world, its rules, and how to respond to them. Our job is to teach them where to stand.

Stepping Up to the Plate

It may be hard to believe, but children really want to behave. They want to be loved, accepted, and find their place in the world, and learning to behave appropriately is a big part of that. The question is, how do we as mothers teach our children the rules? How do we show them where to stand?

The most important part of discipline (after unconditional love, of course) is telling our angels what is expected of them, setting clear expectations, and letting them know what to do in a positive, affirming way. For example, if you want your child to do certain things when he comes in the house, tell him: "Take off your shoes and put your coat on the chair." As he grows older, the expectations can be more complex: "When you come inside, take off your shoes, put them in the basket, hang your coat in the closet, and put your backpack in the kitchen." The fact is, if we want people of any age to do things a certain way, we have to tell them the steps. With children we have to tell them and show them and help them and remind them. Sound exhausting? It is! But it's important. Teaching an angel to do simple tasks now lays the foundation for more complicated tasks in the future (such as driving the family car).

Why are expectations important?

Expectations are the framework of discipline. Children need this framework in order to gain a clear understanding about what they should do, and what they absolutely cannot do—basically, the rules of the game. When children don't behave, it's usually for one of two reasons: either they don't really know what's expected of them, or they know there will be no consequences for inappropriate actions. (We'll talk about consequences later.) As mothers we need this framework, too, because it provides parameters for determining whether or not our children are doing what they should be doing.

To help your child succeed, tell him what to do in simple, specific steps. Make sure he knows there will be consequences for not following those steps.

Why should expectations be specific?

Typically, our expectations start out pretty simple: "Don't talk with your mouth full." "Use a quiet voice in the house." As children get older, however, the expectations become more complex. As a result, sometimes angels don't fully understand what we want them to do or not do.

Look at this example: "Don't talk back to your mother." In this case it's not just what an angel says verbally that is unacceptable; it's also what she communicates with her facial expressions, tone, and body language. Does she understand that she has to watch more than her words? Here's another example: "Don't lie." Does your kindhearted angel understand that lying is wrong even if, in a particular situation, it might protect another person from getting in trouble?

35

Adding to the complexity is the factor of personal desires and preferences. What is a "quiet voice" to you? What does a "clean room" look like in your opinion? Those are parameters you get to set for your child and your home, because you are the mother. But you must be sure to verbalize them. If you really want your angel to do what you ask, you have to be specific.

What are unrealistic expectations?

Then there's the complicating factor of maturity level. What is your angel capable of doing successfully at his age? A five-year-old cannot be expected to make a bed or fold a shirt as well as an eleven-year-old. The younger child simply doesn't have the physical ability to use his hands and arms in the same way. And can we really expect a two-year-old to share a toy without protest, the way we might expect an eight-year-old to do? For developmental reasons, the two-year-old can't get past the thought that she may never get the toy back. Sharing should be on the to-do list for both the two-year-old and the eight-year-old; but in terms of expectations, the *quality* of that sharing will most likely depend upon the child's age.

Unfortunately, we mothers often expect our children to do things they're not capable of doing or can't complete without our assistance. Sometimes perfect little angels just need a little help organizing a task or breaking it down into smaller steps. For example, let's say your angel has been playing for an hour, and toys are everywhere. You say, "Please clean up the toys." Depending on your child's age and attention to detail, he may feel completely overwhelmed and not know where to start. So what does he do? He avoids the task of cleaning up; or, from your perspective, he doesn't listen.

Some children, given the same direction, will put the toys in one big pile; a few will actually put all the pieces in their proper containers and put the containers back in the proper storage space. (I don't have a child like that, do you?) I'm sure we'd all prefer the latter scenario: little toys lined up in perfect order. But even many adults aren't capable of cleaning that way! What is reasonable to expect? Generally speaking, toddlers can be expected to bring us the toys, and we can put them away. Preschoolers can be expected to place toys on shelves and sort small parts with our help. Some elementary-age children may be able to tackle the whole project themselves, but others will need us to at least tell them what step to take first.

*Help your child do what you ask by explaining
specifically what you want, working alongside her if necessary,
and/or breaking down the task into smaller,
more manageable steps.*

What expectations should you set?

A friend once taught me that when it comes to parenting, expectations fall into one of three categories:

- *Safety* (You may not endanger yourself, others, or property.)

- *Respect* (You must respect all people and all property.)

- *Responsibility* (You are responsible for your own actions.)

The simple example of a child coming into the house after school or play has components that fall into each category. "Don't leave your things on the floor. People can trip over them," addresses a safety issue. "We take care of our home by putting things away," addresses a respect issue. "You put away your own shoes, coat, and backpack," is a responsibility matter.

Even toddlers can begin to meet these expectations. For example, I help my toddler take off his shoes when he comes inside, then he waddles over to the basket in the foyer and drops them in. Wouldn't it be easier for me to put his shoes away for him? Yes, and much faster too. But teaching children to meet simple expectations now will help them meet greater ones later.

Let's take a closer look at the three categories of expectations.

Safety:
You May Not Endanger Yourself, Others, or Property

Safety is the most concrete category and a great place to assess our parenting skills. When mothers tell me they can't discipline their children ("I just can't get my child to go to bed" or "My child won't listen to me"), I always raise the safety issue. I ask them, "Do you let your child eat cleaning products?" "Would you let your child stand in front of a moving car?" No, of course not! All moms know how important it is to teach their children not to do these things, because the consequences of doing them are dire.

Well, if we have the ability to teach our perfect little angels not to eat cleaning products, we have the parenting skills to teach them anything—if it's important to us and we think it's worth the effort. If we can teach our angels not to play with matches, we can help them learn other lessons, such as not expecting to buy something every time we go into a store or finishing all their homework assignments before turning on the TV. We really *can* teach our children where to stand and where not to stand.

You have the parenting skills to teach your child anything—if you think it's important enough and worth your effort.

What safety expectations should you set for your child?

Expectations vary from family to family and even parent to parent. I let my children play on the furniture in one of the rooms in my house. Some of my friends think I'm nuts. "They'll get hurt," they say—which is possible. Children and physical activity go together, and children always figure out the most dangerous way to do anything. A mom of preteen boys told me that she was having coffee with a friend one morning and saw something fall past the kitchen window. She went outside to take a peek and realized that the "something" was one of her children. The rest of her boys were lined up on the roof, ready to take the next jump. She was

39

amazed and thankful that no one was hurt. "I've told them lots of things," she said, "but I didn't think I had to specifically tell them not to jump off the roof!"

Back to the sofa: I feel there's minimal risk of serious injury involved in playing on the furniture. "But they'll want to jump on your good furniture," some friends have warned. Actually, my children understand that this one sofa is the only sofa in the world that they can roll around on. They also know that if they even walk into the formal living room without me, there will be serious consequences. You'll see that children will listen and behave if the expectations are clear and age appropriate, and you remind them 101 times.

Your child will listen and behave if your expectations are clear and appropriate—and you remind him of them as often as necessary.

Respect:
You Must Respect All People and All Property

This category is definitely more complex but so important! The world is in need of a lot more teaching about respect. When my mother-in-law recently visited our children's school, I was eager to hear what she thought, because I value her opinion. She raised eight children, and there's not a bad apple in the bunch. Her comment was, "I was so impressed by the way the children opened the door for me." She didn't talk about the merits of the academic program or the cleanliness of the building; she talked about the genuine kindness and respect she received. If only every grandmother would get such treatment at every school, the world would be a much nicer place!

How do you teach your child about respect?

"It's so hard to teach a child to be respectful," I often hear moms complain. That's true. But again, if we can teach our angels not to play with fire (the safety category), we can teach them how to show respect. Start by imagining the type of person you want your child to be when he is a young adult. What do you see? A person that smiles at others, introduces himself with a handshake and a polite greeting, offers a guest refreshments and a comfortable seat? Well then, you have to teach him all those things, and you have to start when he is young. (A good first lesson: teach him as a toddler to always say thank you when someone gives him something.)

Yes, children go through shy stages, and some children are very shy; but encouraging shy angels when they're young will help them feel more comfortable in the world as they grow up. Expecting them to speak up with a thank you or yes, ma'am, or "Hello, Mrs. Peterson," is not too much to ask. For those of us who may be a bit shy ourselves, now is the time to push through our fears, so we can teach our children by example.

At our house we have a lot of talkers, and interruption is a big problem. The expectation that "you may not talk until the other person is finished" is difficult to live up to when you're only seven years old, eager to share a thought, and your four-year-old sister is going on and on and on! So we're working on not interrupting—and being more concise. Think about it: Don't you get annoyed at work or at a social gathering when someone either won't stop talking or constantly interrupts you? I don't want that annoying person to be my child one day! That's why I want my angels to begin now learning where to stand.

What are some simple ways your child can show respect?

Children have unique patterns of growth, and they learn new skills—such as showing respect—at their own pace. Most of them need lots of guidance and reminders through the process. That means that we moms need lots of patience! But by the time our perfect little angels turn six, we can realistically expect them to:

- Say please and thank you
- Take turns
- Tell us their names
- Say hello when they're introduced to someone
- Listen to others speak
- Speak clearly
- Answer the telephone
- Cover their mouths when coughing
- Apologize

- Keep a simple promise or commitment

- Help or offer to help

- Wait a few moments

- Show sympathy

- Begin to empathize

- Show affection

- Play well with other children

- Not hit, pinch, bite, or hurt others

- Share all but special personal items

- Be assertive without being aggressive

- Resolve simple conflicts

- Attempt to resolve more complicated conflicts

- Make friends

Responsibility:
You Are Responsible for Your Own Actions

As adults we know that for everything we say and do, there is a consequence. Some consequences are good, some are not, and some are not at all what we expected. Yet most of us ignore or forget this principle from time to time. "I shouldn't have said that to my husband. I hurt his feelings." "I should have paid the telephone bill instead of using the money to buy that sweater." Being responsible for your own actions at all times is not easy! To give our children the best chance for success, we need to start them out with a limited amount of responsibility at a young age and increase that responsibility as they grow older.

Perfect little angels learn responsibility in four stages: first to *self*, then to *personal belongings*, then to *family*, and then to the *community*. They start with very small steps, such as feeding themselves, dressing themselves, and brushing their own teeth. Over time they begin to take responsibility for their things—putting toys away, placing dirty clothes in the hamper. (These are reasonable expectations for toddlers.) Eventually they learn that responsibility goes beyond self and personal belongings to encompass family and the community.

Why is your child's responsibility to family important?

Today the only responsibilities many children have are attending school, participating in after-school activities, and caring for personal belongings. If they do have household tasks or chores, these family responsibilities come last on the list.

Years ago, responsibility to the family came first. If you didn't collect the eggs from the henhouse, you didn't have food for breakfast. If you forgot to put the animals in the barn at night, you might not be able to find them the next morning. The consequences were immediate and real. We don't have a henhouse behind our home, and I'm truly thankful that I can buy my eggs at the grocery store; still, I do make sure my children help carry in the groceries from the car. They're planning to eat the food too. Even the youngest can tote a loaf of bread.

Depending on their ages, children can be responsible for such tasks as washing their clothes, folding the towels, cleaning the kitchen, and otherwise contributing responsibly to the common family good. In fact, children should be expected to do these things—not just because that's the right thing to do as members of the family, but also because they'll need those skills in the future. I had a roommate in college who had never cooked, didn't know how to put in a load of laundry, and was pretty helpless when it came to even the simplest household chores. How sad!

As moms, we need to empower our children with the skills they need for everyday living. Yes, it's always faster and usually easier for us to do the things that need to be done. But if we take the time to teach these skills to our children, when they're older they will not only be helpful; more importantly, they'll be capable.

Empower your child with the skills he needs for every day.
A child should be expected to do real chores at home for
two reasons: he is an integral member of the family,
and he will need to know those skills later in life.

What responsibilities can you expect your child to take on?

Again, children learn new skills at their own pace. Their responsibilities should start with easier tasks when they're young and become progressively more complex as they grow older. Angels will no doubt need lots of guidance and reminding, but by age six, they should be able to:

- Wash and dry their hands
- Brush their teeth with minimal help
- Get dressed with minimal help
- Feed themselves
- Help to set and clear the table
- Bathe themselves with minimal help
- Tie their own shoes
- Know their full names, phone numbers, and addresses
- Complete one household chore each day, such as making the bed or taking out the garbage
- Help with younger siblings
- Go to bed when they're told to
- Turn off the computer or TV when they're told to
- Follow requests from their parents and teachers
- Have a degree of impulse control
- Begin learning the difference between right and wrong

How can your child be responsible in the community?

The final stage of responsibility is to the community. My husband and I feel strongly about being helpful, volunteering, and doing what we can to improve the quality of life in our community for our family and others. Young children can learn to put their garbage in the trash can at the park; let flowers and plants grow instead of picking them; and only draw on paper, not playground equipment. My family recently visited Ellis Island in New York City. During the renovation of this historical site, the museum uncovered signatures, comments, and drawings that immigrants had long ago written or carved on the columns of the building while they were waiting to be processed. What an interesting insight into an era! What was even more interesting to me, however, was my daughter's comment: "They shouldn't have done that graffiti. I guess they used pens because they didn't have spray paint." I couldn't help but smile. She is learning where to stand.

As children get older, they can help elderly neighbors with chores, stock cans at the food pantry, or participate in citywide clean-ups. They can begin to grasp the concept that to make a community better, everyone has to do their part. If your child takes the first step by baking cookies for a sick neighbor, she's just been responsible for bringing three more smiles in the world: her own, the neighbor's, and yours. Sometimes earning those wings isn't so hard after all!

Here are a few other things our children can do:

- Plant flowers at a local park, nursing home, or library
- Plant a tree or shrub on Arbor Day (the last Friday of April)
- Participate in a community parade or event
- Collect clothing or personal items and donate them to a local shelter

- Make tray favors, scrapbooks, napkin rings, or crafts to donate to a children's hospital or nursing home

- Adopt a grandparent or shut-in to visit on a regular basis

- Help a senior citizen with necessary chores

- Plan or cooperate with paper drives and other recycling efforts

- Present baked or perishable goods to a food bank or to someone in need

- Collect canned goods for a food pantry

- Make greeting cards for people in a veterans' hospital or other healthcare facility

- Make bird feeders for a local park or nature center

- Adopt a serviceperson stationed overseas, collect items he or she may need, and send a gift box

- Donate toys or games to a childcare center or pediatric unit of a hospital

Remember, perfect little angels need the framework that our expectations provide. They need to understand, in specific and affirming ways, what we expect them to do when it comes to the critical issues of safety, respect, and responsibility. But we need to do more than teach them with words; we need to show them by example. That way, when it's their turn to step up to the plate, they will know where to stand.

What can your child learn from misbehavior?

Creating
Teachable
Moments for
Your *Angel*

In the first chapter, we said that a key to disciplining perfect little angels is to think about discipline as a teachable moment and not necessarily a punishable one. Every time our children behave inappropriately, we have a choice. Will we react with anger, impatience, frustration, and punishment driven by our emotional state, or will we take a deep breath and use our children's behavior as an opportunity to create a teachable moment? Creating a teachable moment is not as difficult as it may seem. You simply have to follow these three steps:

- *Make parenting the priority* by stopping what you are doing and going to your child.

- *Capture your child's attention* by making contact at eye level.

- *Diffuse the situation* by validating your child's feelings.

Let's take a closer look at each of these steps.

Making Parenting the Priority

Our perfect little angels inevitably misbehave when we're in the kitchen with a baked chicken in our hands, on the phone with Publisher's Clearinghouse, coming out of the laundry room with a basket full of clean clothes, at the checkout line in the grocery store, driving in a rainstorm, or completely naked and covered with soap in the bathtub. Why are these the perfect times for kiddy chaos? Kids are smart, and they know when we're most likely to be too busy to intervene. But there are more basic reasons too. When we're preparing dinner, they're usually hungry. When we're on the phone, they miss our attention. When we're doing household chores, they're eager for a playmate. When we go shopping for a long time, they get tired. When we're driving, they're anxious to get to their destination. When we're in the bathtub, they're curious about what we're doing and why we seem to enjoy being alone.

So what's a mom to do? Yell "Stop that!" from across the room (or across the house)? Make a mean face in the rearview mirror? Hurl that baked chicken into the playroom? I admit I'm guilty of having done the first two. But no way would I ruin a perfectly good dinner or a clean floor by throwing a chicken!

What's the first thing you should do when your child misbehaves?

The single most important thing we can do when our perfect little angels are acting up is to stop what we are doing and go to them. I know what you're thinking: *You have got to be kidding! I'm going to put down the phone, stop the car, ask the hundred shoppers behind me to wait, or come out of the shower dripping wet?* Yes, and here's why. When we stop what we are doing and go to our children, we are:

- Acknowledging the inappropriate behavior when it happens

- Correcting our children immediately following their actions

- Giving them an opportunity to learn what is right

- Making parenting the priority

Of course, yelling across the room may work—at first. It interrupts the behavior and startles or frightens a child into stopping. But over time that loud mommy voice will begin to fall on deaf ears. Besides, we really don't want our children to fear us, do we? We want them to respect us. More importantly, yelling only takes care of half the discipline equation. Discipline isn't only about stopping inappropriate behavior; it's also about teaching what's appropriate.

*The next time your child does something wrong,
don't yell at her or talk to her from another room.
Stop what you are doing and go to your child.*

Should you raise your voice to your child?

Is there a time for a loud voice? Oh, yes. But we should save that booming voice for situations in which our children may be in danger, and we can't physically get to them in time to keep them from harm. If your child darts from your hand in a busy parking lot, yell "Stop!" He is likely to listen, because the tone of your voice will get his attention. But if he's heard you raise your voice frequently in the course of everyday parenting, he may ignore you. If your child is about to put something unsafe in her mouth, again, yell "Stop!" A loud voice used for safety purposes is not the same as a panicky, frazzled mommy yell. Dangerous situations demand the simplicity of a voice that's loud and in control.

If your angel is about to do something unsafe, and you're not sure you can reach him in time to keep him from harm, say "Stop!" in a loud, controlled voice.

Why is it important for you to physically go to your child?

If we consistently stop and go to our children when they're acting up, they will eventually begin stopping their own inappropriate behavior whenever they see us approaching them—not because they feel threatened or afraid, but because they know we're going to guide them. If we're consistent, sometimes a certain look or a touch on the shoulder will be enough to change the behavior of a toddler who has snatched another child's toy or a school-age child who is being too loud.

"Shouldn't I make my child come to *me*?" you may be asking. "After all, *I'm* the mom." Sounds reasonable. And certainly there are times when our children should come to us—when we call them to wash their hands, to get dressed, to answer a question. How do you feel when someone calls you from the other room or shouts a question down the stairs? Generally speaking, it's more respectful and effective for the person making the request to actually go to the other person. And we all know that the best way to teach children is by example.

As moms we all call out from time to time, "Please come downstairs; it's time for dinner" or "Come to the kitchen, and let's check your homework." But what should we do if our children don't come? Stop whatever we're doing and go to them! It's possible they didn't hear us, didn't understand our request, or didn't realize how quickly we wanted them to respond. And it's also possible they just didn't want to do what they were told. Our best bet for teaching them the difference between inappropriate and appropriate behavior is to stop what we're doing and go to them, wherever they are.

I guarantee you really *will* get your child's attention if you pull the car over to a safe place on the side of the road or turn off the water in the tub and come out of the bathroom in a towel. When it comes to stopping misbehavior, there's something highly effective about seeing a dripping-wet mom heading in your direction! (The last time I did the dripping-wet mom act, the situation was instantly diffused by humor. In my home we've found that moments of laughter are often more valuable teaching times than moments of anger and hostility.)

Capturing Your Child's Attention

Ever try to ask your child a question while she is watching TV? Even a toddler will get a dazed, I'm-in-another-world look when her eyes are glued to the television screen. (That's reason enough to limit television viewing, don't you think?) If you stand between your child and the set, that little head will just bob back and forth trying to see the screen, never even acknowledging your presence. Imagine if you could capture your child's attention like the people on television can! Once I tried putting my face through the back of the television cabinet to tell my children it was time for dinner. I thought my words might have a greater impact that way. They didn't.

Capturing our children's attention is the second step in turning an act of misbehavior into a teachable moment. We can't teach them if they aren't listening!

How can you get your child's attention?

The most effective approach to getting our children's attention is to talk to them at eye level. With young children, this may require getting down on our knees, leaning over, or sitting on the floor. With older children, the best thing may be for us to sit down next to them on the floor or in chairs—whichever is most convenient. Talking to our children at eye level gains their attention, demonstrates our seriousness, shows our respect, and helps our children better understand what we are saying.

We may have to gently guide the faces of our toddlers and say, "Please look at Mommy." With preschoolers, simply moving into their line of vision usually works. However, we may have to say, "Please look at my eyes," or tap a finger next to our eyes if they're particularly upset or distracted.

With school-age children, we may want to ask, "Are you listening to me?" Putting ourselves at eye level is important, but we shouldn't demand that they look directly in our eyes. Eye contact conveys attention and respect, but school-age children are often too embarrassed or too awkward to look us in the eye while they're being reprimanded. It's likely that they're listening, even if they aren't looking at us. We want our children to feel a sense of control, even during disciplinary talks. In this way they maintain their self-respect and are more likely to internalize our advice and make the right decisions in our absence.

Sit down in a chair or on the floor when you are correcting your school-age child. Putting yourself closer to her level conveys respect and concern.

Is your child really listening?

There are many surprising things about children, but one of the most astonishing is how much they hear and remember of our "mommy talks," even when we think they're not listening. Our words of wisdom aren't always taken to heart immediately, and sometimes our instruction is not implemented in a way we find acceptable; but most of the time, in most situations, our children really are listening and learning. And the very best thing we can do as mothers is continue talking and teaching.

Diffusing the Situation

From time to time at the end of a busy mommy day, I feel a bit frazzled and a little on edge. (My husband would probably rewrite that sentence to say, "Every day at the end of the day, my wife is quite frazzled and way over the edge.") I just want someone to say to me, "Wow, I can't believe all the things you did today. It must be tough being a mom." Just hearing those words is so rejuvenating!

During one late-afternoon trip to the grocery store, I noticed that the lady behind me in the express lane was sensing my growing mommy irritation. She didn't lift an eyebrow, even though the checkout sign said Ten Items or Less, and I had fourteen things. Then my oldest child, who is able to read, announced, "You have more than ten, Mommy. You have more than ten." The kind lady looked at me, smiled, and said, "It must be frustrating trying to shop with children."

Immediately my irritation melted, and the tension left my face. Someone understood! Her words didn't change my circumstances, but her understanding, her acknowledgment of my feelings, somehow softened my heart and renewed my energy. It diffused the tension of the situation.

How can you acknowledge your child's feelings?

As moms we definitely like having our feelings validated. So do our children. That's why, when our angels misbehave, it's important that we let them know that we understand their feelings—or at least that we're trying to understand. We can do this by saying something like:

- "I know you wanted the toy, but your sister was playing with it first."

- "Did you feel sad when you didn't get invited to the birthday party?"

- "I know you wanted to make a good grade on the test, but you can't look at someone else's paper."

- "You get frustrated when you don't get to go first."

- "It made you angry when Bobby knocked down your block tower, but you can't hit him."

Children are responsible for their actions and the consequences of those actions, of course. But validating their feelings helps to identify their emotions and diffuse the situation. Being angry and hitting Bobby are two separate things. It's OK to be angry; it's not OK to hit people. A child who feels understood is more likely to listen to guidance, turning the inappropriate action (hitting) into a teachable moment ("Here's what you can and can't do when you're angry"). That's what discipline is all about: identifying the things our children do wrong and teaching them acceptable alternatives.

When your child is misbehaving, tell him you understand
how he is feeling. Name the emotion for him,
and help him respond to that emotion in an acceptable way.

How can you show your child you love her even when you are
disciplining her?

Here's another reason to acknowledge our children's emotions: it
shows them we love them and are concerned about them, even
when they're misbehaving. Our angels need to hear and feel that we
will always love them, even though we may not be happy with their
behavior at that moment. Children who receive this kind of unconditional love from Mommy have more self-respect and self-confidence
than other kids. They have an "I can" attitude that helps them learn
more easily—whether the topic is how to ride a bike, how to read a
book, or the more complex concept of how to behave in a socially
acceptable way. All people, adults and children alike, are more
likely to succeed if they feel competent and supported.

When your child misbehaves,
let him know that you love him
even though you don't like his actions.

58

We have to remember that children don't start certain days with a conscious decision to misbehave or lose control. They don't wake up thinking, "I'm going to try to misbehave today. I'll start by refusing to get dressed. Then toss my breakfast across the room. Break some knickknacks I'm not supposed to touch. And as a grand finale, throw a tantrum in the library." No, children simply get angry and frustrated and tired and impatient through the course of a day—just like we mommies do.

The difference is that as adults, we have the ability to identify our emotions and control our reactions by channeling them in a positive way. Here's what I mean. Suppose you're at the department store, and another mommy has just taken the last on-sale, guaranteed-to-make-you-look-twenty-pounds-lighter swimsuit that you had your eye on first. What do you do? You could (a) run after her and take the bathing suit from her because "it's mine"; (b) hit her and grab the suit; (c) call her a bad name; or (d) complain to the store manager. In your anger, disbelief, and frustration, you'd probably like to do all four. But you don't. You get angry for a moment, think a few not-so-nice thoughts, and move on.

Children haven't learned how to control their emotions and reactions. Often they don't even know what they are feeling. So they take things from others, hit, or call other kids bad names. They don't know the acceptable recourses that are available to them when they've been wronged, how to get what they want in appropriate ways, or how to negotiate the needs of two or more people.

It's our responsibility as moms to teach them these things. That's why we need to take every opportunity to turn our children's acts of misbehavior into teachable moments. As we do this, our angels won't be the only ones learning. We'll be learning too.

What can you say to your child, and how should you say it?

Talking to
Your *Angel*

Have you ever noticed all the different voices we mothers use when we try to discipline our children? See if you recognize any of these as your own:

- *The sugary-sweet voice.* We use this persuasive, I'm-just-the-sweetest-mom-in-the-world-and-you're-my-little-cupcake voice in public places such as church, school, and the homes of friends we want to impress. We figure that the higher we pitch our voice, the more likely it is that our children may actually listen to us while everyone is watching. Meanwhile, we maintain the facade that our kids can do no wrong. We say, "I know you don't want to go home, cupcake, but Mommy has something very special for you if you'll just come along" (the classic bait and bribe).

- *The through-the-teeth voice.* This frustrated, irritated voice is disguised so that we appear to be still smiling and maintaining our sweet, patient mommy image—when in fact we are desperate to get our kids moving without causing a scene. We use the through-the-teeth voice in places where people can see our smiling faces but not necessarily hear what we are saying; for example, in restaurants, grocery stores, and malls. Here's what we say through our teeth: "I've had it. Let's go. You're really going to get it when we get home." (Don't you suppose that children all over the world wonder, "Do I want it? What is it? Have I gotten it before?" Even we moms don't really know what *it* is.)

- *The off-the-Richter-scale voice.* This totally out-of-control, there's-nothing-sweet-left-in-mommy voice is never used in public and rarely witnessed by family and friends. The off-the-Richter-scale voice is very loud, because we think that volume might make up for the fact that our original message was completely ignored. We yell, with more than a tinge of mommy resentment, "I've had enough! No one listens to me. I do so much for you, and you don't even appreciate it!" Children try to leave the room well before this voice has finished its tirade. Often we continue to yell, not realizing that our audience has scattered. But what do we care anyway? No one was listening to us in the first place.

Do any of these voices sound familiar? Don't be too hard on yourself. Probably every mom has used all of these voices at one time or another. But none of the three represent the best way for us to talk to our perfect little angels in teachable moments. If we really want our children to hear what we say and respond positively to our guidance and discipline, we need to:

- Use a natural tone of voice

- Be positive, but firm

- In simple terms explain to our children what they did wrong

Let's take a closer look at each of these keys.

Using Your Natural Tone of Voice

Mommies sometimes have an amazingly high-pitched voice that could break glass. No, most of us aren't opera singers; we're just regular moms who, in times of intense frustration and lost control, bark at our children, thinking that the louder we talk or even yell, the better our children will listen and learn. It rarely works that way, unless our children are temporarily motivated by surprise or fear.

Once I was so desperate for my children to go to sleep that I ranted and raved, yelling the "Rock-a-Bye Baby" lullaby in such a way that the phrase "when the bough breaks" took on a whole new meaning. Finally my two-year-old popped up his little head and commented, "Mommy crazy." All my other children broke out in laughter, and so did I!

At that moment I was experiencing a "mommy meltdown." Been there? Afterward you feel guilty and ashamed, realizing that the only thing you just taught your kids was how to throw a really big tantrum.

The best way to discipline our children is to use our natural tone of voice. After all, we don't want our children to act out of fear or surprise or model our out-of-control yelling. Have you ever been in a situation in which another person constantly yells at you or criticizes you? It's doesn't motivate you to be your best; and although you may comply, you become resentful over time. Children react the same way.

Of course, a few mommy meltdowns probably go with the territory of motherhood. But loud talking or yelling should not be the norm. If we always resort to yelling, we'll forget what our natural tone of voice sounds like. (Kind of like my natural hair color—I haven't seen it for so long, I've forgotten what it looks like.) By talking to our children in a normal voice, firm when necessary, we'll help them maintain their self-respect, their motivation to learn, and their eagerness to comply. We'll also be better role models. Besides, even dog-training books suggest that puppy owners stop yelling at their little charges and lose the harsh tone. Hey, if we're supposed to speak respectfully to dogs, it only makes sense that we should talk to our children that way!

When you are upset with your child, try not to yell or raise your voice. Use a positive, firm, natural tone.

Being Positive, but Firm

Of course, using a natural tone of voice doesn't mean using a monotone voice. In normal, everyday conversation we convey surprise, frustration, doubt, or seriousness not only by the content of our message, but also by our inflection. Think of yourself in a social or business situation. There are times when you are firm, and your voice reflects that, but you don't resort to yelling, right? With children, too, we can be firm without upping the volume. We don't need to scream to teach.

I'll be honest: I can tend to be a screamer at the end of a long day with my children. I've found, however, that my frantic appeals are rarely met with cooperation. My husband, on the other hand, can walk in the door and take what I call the "police officer approach": "Put down the ball and step away from the window." "Eat your green beans. Don't play with your food." "Get off your brother. Tell him why you're mad." Remarkably, the children comply! His reprimands are positive yet firm. Of course, he's not with the children all day. But I'm learning a lot from him.

As the old adage goes, "It's not what you say, but how you say it." For better or worse, our voices can impact our disciplinary exchanges with our children, and the intent of our message can get lost in the delivery. Sometimes our loud, shrill voices fall upon deaf ears; other times it's our uncertain, tentative voices that are ignored. We can be firm without going ballistic. We can be positive without giving in. The key is paying attention to both factors: what we say *and* how we say it.

Explaining What Your Child Did Wrong

Telling our children what they did wrong is something we moms often do—but we don't necessarily do it well. We tend to over generalize, get caught up in the moment, and let our own emotions and frustrations blur the real intent of our interactions with our children: "He's always running around." "She constantly talks back." "My child never listens to me." "He can't stay focused on anything." Those probably aren't fair statements about any child.

Children don't always act like perfect little angels. As we've said, they're trying to figure out how the world works and where they fit. In the process, they test the limits, muddy the waters, and drive us crazy. That's their job. And that's where mothering comes in—the constant guiding, constant reminding, and constant reinforcing that helps our angels know what they can do and what they can't do. Having respectful conversations with our children, loving them, trying to understand their feelings, and giving them acceptable alternatives are all effective methods of discipline and guidance. But ultimately we have to tell our children what they did wrong; otherwise, they will never know.

Why should you tell your angel what she should do before telling her what she shouldn't do?

For most of us, it's more natural to tell our children all of the no's than all of the yes's—all of the things they *can't* or *shouldn't* do rather than all of the things they *can* and *should* do. But that's not good parenting strategy. When our children misbehave, rather than starting out by telling them what they did wrong, we should tell them what they can and ought to do; that is, the positive action or choice they should make in the situation. Think how much more our angels would learn if we were constantly reminding them of the right things to do! By reinforcing the positive first, we teach our children what's acceptable. *Then* we can tell them, in specific and simple language, what they cannot do:

- "Put your feet on the floor. You may not climb on the table."

- "Stay in bed. You may not get out."

- "Please tell me where you are going. You can't be out without my knowing."

- "Tell your brother why you are angry. You may not hit him."

It takes a lot of practice to think and speak this way to our kids. But the results are well worth it.

When you are correcting your child's behavior, state what she is allowed to do first, and then follow with what she did wrong.

How do you tell your child what he did wrong without generalizing?

When we approach misbehavior, we have to remember: it's all about the *what*, not the *who*. Our displeasure is with the actions of the child, not the child. We want our children to walk away from disciplinary moments knowing they made a wrong choice, but that we still love them. Throughout childhood, children are constantly corrected, as they should be; but we need to guide their behavior in a way that helps them gain and maintain self-respect and self-confidence. We want to raise them up, not break them down.

We usually don't intend any harm, but sometimes we have a tendency to say things like, "If you cared about your sister, you wouldn't fight with her." "How many times do I have to tell you to clean up your mess?" "Why would you eat a snack before dinner? What's the matter with you?" (If our children actually answered these rhetorical questions—"I ate the cupcake because I'm starving, and I like cupcakes better than fish sticks"—we'd really go nuts!)

Instead of generalizing, state what your child did wrong by specifically telling him what you know or observed. Avoid being judgmental, preachy, or vindictive. Don't say, "I told you so." Just assert the facts: "You called your sister stupid-head." "You didn't put your clothes in the hamper." "You ate a cupcake before dinner."

Angel Tip

Be specific when you tell your child what he did wrong. He honestly may not know! Instead of saying, "You made a mess," say, "You took all of Mommy's books off the shelf."

What can you say to your perfect little angel when she's flown off course?

When our children misbehave, we can correct and teach them by following these four steps:

- *Say, "I understand that . . ."* (Validate your child's feelings or efforts.)

- *Say, "Please (do) . . ."* (Tell your child the correct behavior or action.)

- *Say, "Please don't . . ."* (Tell your child what she did that was wrong or inappropriate.)

- *Say, "Because . . ."* (Explain the consequences of the inappropriate behavior or choice.)

Here's an example: "*I understand that* you like to climb, but please put your feet on the floor. *Please don't* climb on the table, because the table is for eating."

"*I understand that* you are angry because Bobby knocked down your blocks, but *please* use your words to tell him you are angry. *Please don't* hit people, *because* hitting hurts."

"*I understand that* you are tired and want to go home, but *please* sit in the shopping cart. *Please don't* stand up again, because you may fall and get hurt."

"*I understand that* you want to watch TV, but *please* turn the TV off when this show is over and do your homework. *Please don't* wait until later, *because* you will be tired, and you won't get your homework completed."

Is it really possible to talk to your child like this?

I know what you're thinking: *Your examples sound good on paper, but by the time I say all those things, my child will be in college.* It may not be necessary for you to use all four phrases in every situation, especially when you first start out. And certainly during moments of extreme frustration, impatience, or exhaustion, you may forget to use one or two or all of them. When that happens, just get some rest, then get back on track. Eventually you'll be able to follow all four steps more naturally and spontaneously in more and more circumstances.

Try adding one step at a time, and eventually work up to all four. Your motivation will increase as you discover how effective these steps can be. Even though I've listed it as the second step, try starting with *Please (do)*. When we focus on telling our children what to do, not just what not to do—by using more dos than don'ts—our interactions with them are more positive, and we find that our days are filled with more teachable moments than punishable ones.

Of course, we can't eliminate all of our children's wrong choices. Mistakes are a natural part of being a child. But by adopting these four steps, using a natural tone of voice, and speaking to our children in a way that is both positive and firm, we can respond more positively to misbehavior. And we can develop a framework for talking to our angels that will help them learn, grow, and eventually, fly.

How can you help your child learn self-control?

Setting
Your Angel
to *Listen*

Every evening when my husband comes home from work, he asks me jokingly, "So who won today?" He's not talking about the Yankees versus the Braves. He's talking about the children versus me. Usually he can guess the answer by the condition of the house and the look on my face—or the absence of any look at all: that wide-eyed, blank stare that leaves him wondering, *Is anyone in there?* I'm in there, all right. I'm just a bit shell shocked.

Who won? You know the answer! Isn't it amazing how a three-year-old child who refuses to follow direction can reduce an otherwise fairly competent, sane adult into a mommy who pleads, begs, bribes, threatens, cries, and yells? I'd rather wrestle an alligator than a kid who doesn't want to get in his car seat.

The Meanest Mommy in the World

I remember the day my husband asked my four-year-old, as he tossed her into the air, "How much do you love Daddy?"

"A-hundred-million-smillion-and-twenty," she replied with adoring eyes.

"And how much do you love Mommy?" I asked, expecting to hear "a-hundred-million-smillion-and-twenty-one."

She pointed her little finger in the air. "One," she said.

After that answer, I shouldn't have been surprised when my six-year-old told me the other night, "You're the meanest mommy in the world." Thank goodness the baby can't talk yet!

The truth is, even though I haven't slept much in the last seven years, I'm not the meanest mommy in the world. But if I were, I'd have a time clock in the kitchen, and at 8:00 p.m. sharp (7:30 on holidays), I would punch out. Shift over. Mommy's off duty. If at 8:15 a wee, small voice called, "Mommy!" I would reply, "She's not here!" If I were the meanest mommy in the world, there'd be no more boo-boo kissing, snack fixing, or answering questions about where everything in the house is. ("It's under your bed by the doll with no hair, in front of the half-eaten jelly bean.") I would never, ever let my children watch TV unless the show was super-educational ("The Life Cycle of the Common Housefly," for example). My kids' toys would consist of cleaning equipment and school supplies; and if I wanted to be a little less mean, I might allow them to clean out the lint in the dryer vent. If I were the meanest mommy in the world, I would give out absolutely no kisses, only handshakes for a job well done; and I would serve only green food (broccoli, green beans, lima beans, and spinach).

But like I said, I'm not the meanest mommy in the world. I'm just like every other mommy. I get tired, lose my patience, lay down the law, threaten to do things I'll never do, and act like a child myself. I love and discipline, cook and clean, play and hug. Yes, I do make my children eat green food, clean their rooms, do their schoolwork, and turn off the TV. But I never stop loving them, and I never, ever run out of kisses.

Guiding Your Little Angel

All mommies at one time or another resort to pleading, begging, bribing, threatening, crying, and yelling when their children won't listen to them. And all of us end up learning the same thing: when it comes to guiding our kids and getting them to do what we say, none of those tactics work in the long run.

So what can we do? There's no magic solution, but there are some strategies we can employ—some methods designed to help our children listen to us, understand the consequences of not listening, and develop self-control.

What is listening anyway?

If your eight-year-old child finally picks up his backpack after you ask him for the third time, is that listening or not? If you tell your five-year-old that it's time to go home, but it takes fifteen minutes to get her out of the park, is that listening or not? In both situations, probably not. We all want our children to do what we say, and to see them start moving at our first request is a reasonable expectation and a legitimate mommy goal.

Of course, toddlers often need to be asked several times before they really listen to a particular command, because that's how they learn. Think about it. They like to read the same *Pat the Bunny* book 100 times, sing "Twinkle, Twinkle, Little Star" 102 times, and wear the same clothes for days. They need repetition! Preschoolers, too, need lots of reminding. By school age, however, children usually know what we expect of them. We shouldn't have to tell them twice (although many times we do).

Should your school-age child respond the first time you ask him to do something?

Should older children be expected to listen the first time? Yes. But if they seem to be struggling with this concept, it's a good idea for us to take a look at our own behavior to see if we're laying out too many requests in a row, changing the rules of the game, or simply interrupting our children's activities without warning. In the adult world, there are warnings for speeding tickets, probations for first offenses, and "I'm sorrys" for unkind words. We need to make sure we're not being unfair to our children by expecting too much and setting them up to fail.

Should you want and expect perfect obedience?

Actually, no. All children are perfect little angels, but that doesn't mean that all of their choices, actions, and behaviors are going to be perfect. Besides, there's a lesson—a teachable moment—inherent in every act of disobedience. If our children never confronted us, never disobeyed, or never showed a lack of respect, how and when would we have the opportunity to teach them about conflict resolution, admitting mistakes, and forgiveness?

I think it's better to expect our children to strive for behavior that is excellent, not perfect. Angels need to grow up in a consistent, predictable environment that sets a high standard and makes them accountable for their actions but that also allows for mistakes, forgiveness, and learning.

Why are you often surprised by your child's misbehavior?

As mothers we have a pretty good sense of how the world works; and although we may not always know what's going to happen next, we have a good idea of the possibilities. We also have a well-developed sense of time. We know how long it takes to nuke frozen chicken nuggets to perfection, how soon we'll get up to the drive-through window based on the number of cars in line, and the exact number of minutes necessary to get to school on time (assuming no one has to go to the bathroom at the last minute).

Our children, on the other hand, haven't experienced and don't know all the possibilities or outcomes of certain actions. They don't have a mature concept of time, and their grasp of cause-and-effect relationships is limited. "I squeeze my baby sister, and she cries." "I beg for candy at the store, and Mommy gives in." That's as far as their attention span takes them.

What does this have to do with discipline? We mothers are usually thinking two or three cause-and-effect steps ahead. Our children, on the other hand, don't always know what will happen next or what to expect. Sometimes when our children do certain things, we're quite astonished. "Why would you swing that toy around? Didn't you know you'd hurt someone?" Did she know? Maybe yes, maybe no, depending upon her age and experience. Anticipation is part of the mothering role. As moms we know when a cup is too close to the edge of the table and likely to fall. We know when it's time to wind down for bed. Our children don't have the same sense of time and consequence.

As a result, children are often surprised and frustrated when we interrupt their games or suddenly transition into another activity. We can alleviate some of their frustration by preparing them for the change: "After you go down the slide, we're leaving the park."

"When we get home, we are having a snack and then doing homework."

"You have five more minutes to play, and then you're going to clean up your toys."

"In five minutes, we're going to go inside and get ready for dinner."

Whenever possible, give your child a five-minute warning before moving on to the next activity. She'll make the transition more easily if she knows what to expect.

Let's say we've given the warnings. We've told our angels what to expect. Yet they still won't listen and do what we say. What can we do? Here are three options to try:

- Impose logical consequences.

- Offer choices.

- Redirect attention.

Let's look at each of these more closely.

Imposing Logical Consequences

Logical consequences are simple and direct. If our children won't do something the way they've been told to do it, they can't do it: "If you refuse to turn the TV off after your show, you can't watch TV tomorrow."

"If you argue with your brother, you can't play with your brother for the rest of the day."

"If you come home late for lunch, you can't go out to play in the afternoon."

"If you write on the walls instead of on paper, you can't use the markers."

Logical consequences sound so simple. Why are they so hard?

Logical consequences represent the most sensible response to inappropriate behavior. Unfortunately, they're the most difficult to implement, especially in our I'm-a-busy-mommy-and-I-don't-have-time-to-deal-with-misbehavior world. Logical consequences take time and effort. It's so much quicker and easier to yell at our kids from another room or threaten to take their toys away forever. It's even easier to do nothing at all—that is, until we reach the I-can't-take-it-anymore phase, which really confuses our children. When we finally show up to correct them, they look up at us as if to say, "I was banging on the table with this book for a long time. Why is it bothering you now?"

"This wasn't too loud ten minutes ago."

"You didn't seem so concerned the last time I went out with those friends."

How do you implement the logical consequences strategy?

For logical consequences to work, we have to be willing to do what it takes to make our expectations clear and then follow through on a consistent basis. For example, when you give your child markers, tell her clearly, "Write on the paper and not on anything else." Then set her up to succeed, not fail. If you think she'll probably have trouble following your direction, stay with her. If you're working in the kitchen, and you think she's likely to go off the page (even unintentionally), keep her and the markers in the kitchen. Don't give her the markers at all if you're not up to helping her learn how to use them appropriately. And if she intentionally writes on things other than paper, despite your best efforts to help her, by all means, take the markers away—even if the results are cries and protests. Follow through, and be consistent. Eventually she'll learn.

If you don't have the time or energy to help your child in a particular activity, or you're not willing or able to stop and offer guidance if necessary, don't start the activity.

Here's another example of the logical-consequences method. Before your children begin playing, tell them, "When you and your brother play together, I expect you to use a regular tone of voice to work out your differences. You may not yell at each other or hit each other. If you do, you may not play together." By making this statement, you've set up a clear expectation, told your children what they can and can't do, and explained what will happen if they don't listen. Now you just have to follow through the first time you hear raised voices! It usually only takes a few times of Mom actually doing what she says she's going to do before children understand there will be consequences if they misbehave.

Offering Choices

With this second strategy, we give our children a choice between two activities that we propose: "It's time to eat dinner. Do you want to put your seat beside your sister or me?" "It's cold outside. Do you want to put on your blue sweater or your red jacket?" Offering choices not only guides our angels' behavior, it shows that we respect them because we're giving them a role in the process. It also helps them to learn to make decisions and develop independence. To be effective, however, the choices approach requires that we follow a few rules:

- Only offer choices you are willing to accept.

- Limit the choices to two.

- Offer small choices to small children and bigger choices to older children.

- Be open to your child proposing a third choice, but don't feel you have to accept it.

Why does offering choices work?

As mothers, we're in charge. We get to decide the activity or chore that our children must do. But by offering choices, we give them some control over their participation, some flexibility. Our children must do what we say, but they have the freedom to choose between two alternatives in order to accomplish it: "We're cleaning up the playroom. Do you want to put away the blocks or the puzzles?" With older children or more challenging children who have a tendency to answer no to either choice, we may have to state our request more firmly: "We're cleaning up the playroom. You must pick up the blocks or the puzzles. Which do you want to put away?"

Offer your child no more than two choices, but consider an alternative if she suggests it.

Some of my favorite nighttime choices are: "Do you want to go to bed or read for a little while?" "Do you want to go to bed or help me clean the kitchen?" "Do you want to go to bed or . . . ?" Children of all ages inevitably choose the *or* over going to bed, if going to bed means lights out. We mommies need to make sure the second option is something worthwhile!

How do you get your child to comply with his choice?

Offering our children a choice sounds easy enough, but how do we get them to actually do what they choose? *Consistency.* If we always require our children to clean up after play, they will learn that cleanup is a part of the play process and not a debatable option. The same goes for "homework before TV," "no candy when we go to the grocery store," and any other reasonable expectations we set.

Of course, we have some leeway in the quality of response we expect. Take cleaning up: For some of us, just pushing the toys into the corner somewhere in the vicinity of the toy shelf is good cleaning. For others, nothing will do except placing the toys exactly in the correct spot above the label on the shelf. Either is OK—if it's OK with us! We just need to make our expectations clear and take into consideration our children's developmental ability to do what we ask. A clean home and good organization is important, but so is relaxing enough to enjoy the fun our children are having.

Should you give your child a choice about everything?

I can hear you thinking, *Why give a choice at all? Shouldn't children just listen?* Sure. We should expect our children to listen to us, whether we give them choices or not. But ultimately, discipline is about teaching. Offering our children some control over their behavior and actions from time to time provides a foundation for them to learn how to make right choices when we're not around to decide for them.

CHAPTER SIX

Redirecting Attention

The third strategy for getting our children to listen is called redirection. With this approach, when our children are upset or acting out, we divert their attention, guide them to stop or leave what they're doing, and encourage them to find interest in something else. Basically, we direct them to a new activity, and we no longer allow them to do what they were doing before: "You can't play with blocks if you throw them. Here, you can throw this ball outside." Redirection takes energy, creativity, and the ability to remain calm. It's kind of like Mom as cruise director: we're responsible for fun and excitement and keeping everyone busy.

When your child is fussing about something in public, try diverting her attention by guiding her to find interest in something else.

How do you use redirection?

The redirection strategy can be used in virtually any situation or place. In restaurants: "Count how many chicken dishes they have on the menu." "Name all the things you see that are the color blue." In playgroups: "I know you want to play with that toy, but Katie has it right now. Look at this toy. It spins so fast." Riding in the car: "What do you think is in that truck?" When I'm in the car with squabbling siblings and feeling desperate, I like to call out, "Look at that!" with a high degree of excitement. Heads turn, eyes pop, and the kids start talking about something they see—when, in fact, I saw nothing at all.

A good way to redirect our children is with a change of scenery. When it feels like chaos inside your house, take your child outside. Put sunscreen on both of you, bundle up if it's cold, find raincoats and boots if necessary—whatever it takes to get out in the fresh air for a while. I've found that unless my children are tired or hungry, going outside is a cure-all for everything. And I feel better too.

When your angel is out of control or headed that way, change your location. Take your child to another room, walk around, or go outside.

How does redirection help your child regain self-control?

Have you ever been in an argument that begins to escalate quickly? Sometimes you just need to walk away, take a break, and regain your self-control. That's you redirecting yourself. Have you ever waited in a restaurant for a meal that seems to be taking forever, and the waitress brings you another loaf of bread or an order of drinks or a free appetizer? That's the restaurant redirecting you, trying to take your mind off how hungry and impatient and possibly angry you are.

Then there are the everyday disasters: the car won't start, the electricity goes off, the baby gets sick. Sometimes we mommies throw a tantrum or cry or just sit like zombies. We're trying to regain our self-control. And after a few minutes, we usually do. Then we amend our plans and start to assess what we can do about the situation. We redirect ourselves.

When things don't go the way our children want them to, they, too, may throw a tantrum or cry or refuse to listen to us. The difference between children and mommies is, children don't have the skills yet to redirect themselves and regain self-control on their own. We have to guide them. For example, if you're out shopping and you see your child beginning to lose control because she wants another ice-cream cone or outfit or toy, by all means, leave the store. Help her to regain control by redirecting her attention in another setting. Depending upon her maturity level and the situation, you may find that you can go back into the store in just a few minutes.

Doesn't redirection reward your child's misbehavior?

Sometimes it may seem that diverting our children's attention with a fun activity or by taking them outside actually rewards them for acting out. However, redirection, like all good discipline strategies, is a learning tool. Children are still trying to learn to control their emotions and behaviors. With redirection we're helping them regain self-control, and from there they can start to behave again. It's like helping your child get back on his bike after falling off. You don't say, "Oh, forget it! You're never going to learn to ride a bike. Why do I bother?" No, you help him get up, dust him off, and encourage him to try again.

But what if your child acts out to get attention?

Children definitely want our attention and approval. These are valid needs, and we must be sure that we are giving our children enough of both. If we notice that our children are constantly acting out in the car, when we're on the phone, or when we're with other children, it's worth considering the possibility that they may need more attention from Mommy.

Children are smart, and they will work to get what they want and find out just how far they can stretch their boundaries. Some children quickly learn that acting out gets attention—negative attention, perhaps, but they figure, *That's OK with me.* When we redirect our children by showing interest in them and engaging them in another activity, we are giving them the attention they want, but not in a way that gives in to misbehavior. We're giving them attention that teaches appropriate behavior.

Sure, there are times when kids just have to wait. We can't always stop what we're doing. If I gave everyone in my family all the attention they asked for every day, I'd be dead or in a home for burned-out, overachieving mommies. Here's my goal: to do my best every day to give my kids what they need, including my attention. Each day is not the same; the needs of my children aren't the same; and my emotional and physical ability to give is different at different times. But when I do my best to spend time with my children daily—not just around them, but really *with* them—I know I have accomplished something.

Perhaps you're thinking, "I'm tapped out. I have no more to give." Try looking at how you spend your time, and figure out ways to carve out private moments with your child, even if it's when you're tying his shoes and zipping up his coat. If you're thinking, "I should spend more time with my child," then do! We mommies can get so busy keeping the house clean, working, and running errands that we forget to really *be* with our children. Sometimes mommies need a little redirection too.

When you're on the cell phone and your child grabs at your arm and whines for you, ask yourself, "What is more important in my life than raising my child? Nothing, right?" Then hang up the phone and talk to her! If you must, tell her, "Let Mommy finish this call, and then I will talk to you." Then finish the call quickly, and start enjoying the company of your child.

Redirection has one additional benefit, and this one is for mommies: it's a terrific way to rediscover the simple things in life—the beauty of the sky, the smell of homemade waffles, the feel of soft grass on bare feet. So practice saying, "Look at that!" with excitement and enthusiasm. "Smell that!" "Feel that!" Then open your eyes (and the rest of your senses) to all the wonderful things you can see, learn, and experience in the company of your perfect little angel.

What can you do when your child doesn't do what you say?

Setting Consequences for a Misbehaving *Angel*

We've talked a lot about approaching our children's acts of misbehavior as teachable moments instead of punishable moments. But what if we've done everything we can think of to validate, comfort, and guide our kids, and they still don't listen? Those are the times for consequences. And consequences, to be effective, must be consistently enforced. We must follow through and do what we say we're going to do; otherwise, our children will learn that the consequences we impose on negative behavior are unpredictable—or worse, they're predictable, because they're never implemented.

As our perfect little angels grow up, they continue to experiment with all types of responses to mommy requests, trying to figure out what their limits are and how far they can push the boundaries we've set. They're not the only ones who push boundaries, however. I'm a mother, and I still do. I'll be honest:

Sometimes when I'm late, I go just a little over the speed limit and hope that I don't get a ticket, even though I know I'm disobeying the law. And I'm notorious for handing in paperwork late at the preschool. If the school were to put its foot down and say, "No field trip for you and your child. Your permission slip was late," or "Your child can't come to school until we have a copy of her updated medical report," I'd stop pushing the boundaries. But I can, and so I do.

Pushing boundaries, I think, is part of human nature. But in order to grow into responsible adults, children need to learn that there are some boundaries that can't be pushed. There are some limits that cannot be breached. Punishment in the form of appropriate consequences is what helps our little angels learn how to make good choices and wise decisions in the future.

Here's how it works: Let's say the last time your school-age child was defiant with his teacher, you kept him from going Rollerblading with his friends that afternoon. Now he's back in school, and the teacher asks him to finish his seatwork before going to play on the computer. His first thought is to hop out of his seat and head to the computer, but experience reminds him, "The last time I didn't listen to the teacher, Mom made me miss Rollerblading. I think I'll just finish my work and then play." Your child learned from the consequences of past punishment. And that's what we mommies want—to keep our angels flying straight, especially when we're not around to guide them.

What kinds of consequences are most effective? Basically, they fall into three categories:

- *Time-out.* With this approach, we don't allow our children to do anything for a certain period of time. For younger children: "You have to share the cards. Let's take a break for a while. Sit down over here." For older children: "You told me that I'm ruining your life. You have to speak to me respectfully. Go to your room until I say you can come out."

- *"Stay with me."* In this case, we have our children stay by our sides as we continue our work or activity. For younger children: "You keep throwing the book. Stay with me while I fold the laundry." For older children: "You rolled your eyes when I asked you to pick up your shoes. You need to stay with me in the kitchen for a while."

- *Takeaway.* Here we don't allow our children to do an activity they want to do. For preschool children, takeaways are not appropriate, as I'll explain later. But for older children: "You haven't completed your homework. You can't watch TV tonight." "You continued to argue with your sister and pulled her hair. You may not go to your friend's birthday party."

Let's look at each of these consequences in more detail.

Consequence #1: Time-Out

Are you thinking, "Isn't time-out an overused, old-fashioned, ineffective way of guiding a child's behavior?" I tried to come up with a trendy new name for it, but the only thing I could think of was Fresh Start, and that sounded like laundry detergent. When used appropriately, time-out is very effective. Sometimes the best consequence for children is to make them take a break and do nothing for a few minutes. Children who are out-of-control, repeatedly defiant, or hurting themselves or others *need* to stop what they're doing. They need to be separated from their actions.

Should time-out feel like punishment? Sure. Should it be humiliating? Absolutely not. Don't put your child in a special chair in the corner of the room for everyone to see and snicker at. In colonial days, that would be like putting him in the stocks. (Remember those old contraptions in the center of the town square that a person was forced to put his arms and head through?) Instead, have your child sit down on the sofa or in a chair or on his bed in his room. By making him sit down, you're sending a clear message of "stop." You're teaching and physically showing him that what he was doing will not be allowed.

If you want a particular behavior to stop immediately, put your child in a chair. Send an older child to her room.

After all, children are just beginning to learn how to recognize their emotions and control their reactions. Time-out can help. When kids are experiencing anger, frustration, confusion, and willfulness, a few minutes of sitting still gives them a chance to refocus their attention and opens the door for us to teach them about self-control, patience, and tolerance. (Of course, we mommies are still learning these things too. If it were acceptable for me to ram the wheels of my shopping cart into the heels of the person in front of me who is spending way too much time selecting pickles, I'd probably do it. But I'm getting better at controlling my grocery-store rage.)

What should you do to assist your child when he is in time-out?

After we have separated our children for a few minutes by using the time-out method, we should go to them and comfort them. We may want to ask, "Do you need a hug?" Some children will dissolve into tears and reach for our support. Others may respond with a puzzled look, as if to say, "I thought you were mad at me for pulling my sister's hair." At that point we can reassure them by saying, "I love you even though I am angry at you for hurting your sister. I want to help you to stop hurting others." It's important that we differentiate between the angel and the not-so-angelic behavior. This is the time to make clear, "I love you even though I am not pleased with what you did."

Children need to understand that mommies don't cast their children away when they make mistakes. We don't put them in the corner for a lifetime. We love them. We're here to support our children and to help them—especially when they make wrong choices. When they're on the wrong path, that's when it takes all the compassion, energy, love, support, and discipline we can give. Being a mommy is a tough job!

*After you discipline your child, go to her and reassure her that
you love her even though you are angry. Differentiate between
your approval of her and your disapproval of her action.*

How long should you put your child in time-out?

How long should time-out last? Some experts recommend one
minute for every year of age. A two-year-old would sit for two
minutes, for example. Find a second hand on a watch and time
two minutes. It's a long time. Really, try it!

Are you thinking, "My two-year-old should be able to sit for
two minutes. That's hardly punishment"? Well, it's certainly not
cruel or inappropriate. But time-out is not meant to be a battle in
itself. If trying to keep our children in time-out becomes more of
an issue than the reason we put them there, what will we really
gain? Of course, some children have to be physically held in time-
out to help them regain control. Others go willingly—but then,
they're typically the kids who don't get much time-out anyway.

Back to the question "How long is enough?" It depends. What
are we trying to accomplish? Basically, time-out is like a giant
stop sign. We want it to be long enough to get our children to
stop misbehaving and start listening to us. For toddlers, redirection is a more effective strategy than time-out. But preschoolers
should be able to sit for a few minutes, and school-age children
should be able to sit longer, depending upon the message we want

to send. We may have to put our children back in time-out if they continue the same wrong behavior when they get up.

I actually set a timer to avoid leaving my kids in time-out forever. It's a major mommy power rush to have all my kids sitting still without a word! I could get lost in it—throw in a couple of loads of laundry, grab a cup of coffee, chat on the phone. But I'm not trying to be a prison warden. I'm trying to be a teacher. The timer helps me remember my children are there. It also eliminates countless calls of "Can we get up yet?" Timer goes off, play resumes.

Who is in control?

Of course, parents should have the ultimate authority when guiding their children. But discipline is not about power and control. Discipline is about empowering our children and teaching them self-control. My children aren't slaves or prisoners or hostages. I'm not trying to scare them into good behavior. Fear is not a good motivator in the long run; and besides, I'm not particularly scary. What am I going to do? Ground them forever? "You'll never leave this house again, young lady!" That would be bad for me, because I don't want my kids sticking around forever. I already know what I'm planning to do with their rooms when they're all out of here: a studio for writing, a craft room, more storage space . . .

If we turn discipline into a power play, we set ourselves up as competitors against our own children. Then, when we successfully control our kids, we're the winners—and that makes them losers. I don't want my children to be losers! I want them to be winners too. I want win-win scenarios.

What are you trying to teach your child?

My hope, my goal, is that somewhere in the brains of each of my children, I have created a "mommy memory bank" of good advice—a storehouse of wisdom about what to do and how to act in any given situation. Here's how it works: Child notices he has something in his nose. Child goes to put finger in nose. Mommy memory bank kicks in: *Use a tissue. Go to the bathroom to do that. And whatever you do, never ever put anything that comes out of your nose in your mouth.* Child proceeds to bathroom to get a tissue.

Here's another example: Adolescent child wants candy in store, but doesn't have any money. Adolescent puts hand on candy bar and starts to put it in his pocket. Mommy memory bank kicks in: *Taking something without paying for it is stealing. You could go to jail for doing that.* Adolescent puts candy down and leaves store.

Here's another: Teenage child of driving age has a slight fender bender with a parked car and wants to leave the scene. Teenager begins to drive away. Mommy memory bank kicks in: *When you do something wrong, it's always easier in the long run to face the consequences than to lie or not tell someone.* Teenager puts a note on the parked car and grumbles something under his breath about his mother.

Time-out, I'm convinced, is one of the keys to creating an

effective mommy memory bank. If our children stay with us until they are eighteen years old and then live to be eighty or so, they will be with us for about 25 percent of their lives. What kind of people will they be for the other 75 percent of their lives? What decisions will they make? The answer depends a great deal on our willingness to guide, teach, and discipline them now.

Consequence #2: "Stay with Me"

For the most part, infants, toddlers, and even preschoolers are constantly by Mommy's side, within arm's reach, just a nose blow away, and certainly within sight. As children become older, however, they become more independent, caring for much of their own hygiene (or not caring), and spending more and more time playing independently at home or in activities with friends away from home. When our kids reach this stage, it's easy for us to be around them without actually interacting or talking with them. Yet children of all ages need to see our actions and hear our words if they're going to learn how to act appropriately in the world. That's why the "stay with me" method of discipline can be so effective.

How does the "stay with me" method work?

The "stay with me" strategy works well with children of all ages, but especially school-age children. In the "stay with me" method, we require our children to shadow our every move—to hang out with us even though, from a mothering perspective, they don't require our constant attention. When my two daughters argue, I usually separate them or let them figure out their differences on their own, depending upon the severity of the situation. Sometimes, instead of sending them to their rooms or somewhere else (the dog kennel would be nice), I use the "stay with me" method and require them to follow me as I go about completing chores, errands, and caring for their younger siblings. They don't get to just follow me, however; they're also required to help and talk.

The next time your older child misbehaves, instead of sending him to his room, keep him by your side. Have him shadow you.

Shouldn't you separate your child from you when he misbehaves?

Of course, it would be much easier for me to just separate myself from the arguing. Who wants to be around misbehaving children? But "stay with me" has so many benefits. For one, it works as a consequence, because it's not usually what my children want to do. (And I thought I was so much fun!) Secondly, it gives me an opportunity to reconnect with my more independent older children, opening the door for me to talk to them and teach them about all sorts of things. Typically we'll talk briefly about their argument, then move on to laundry or picking up sticks in the yard or making dinner. More times than not, a difficult, upsetting, and tense moment turns into a fun, teachable, family-oriented one.

Does "stay with me" reward inappropriate behavior?

Absolutely not! Does it teach children to remove themselves from potentially volatile situations, learn to compromise and argue appropriately, and experience forgiveness and reconciliation? Absolutely yes.

There are times when my children hang out with my husband and me because they want to be with us: at mealtime, when we gather around the fireplace for a game, when we do a chore together or something fun as a family. But "stay with me" is different. This is something they have to do as a result of inappropriate behavior. They are required to be with me, even though they'd prefer to do something else. There is no choice.

It's easier to teach your child if you keep him with you than if you send him away in punishment.

What can you teach your child if he is with you?

Remember that old last resort for teachers, "You're going to the principal's office"? So many of our discipline techniques involve separating our children from us, at least for a time. But if we want to teach our children those things that are most important, if we want to whisper in their ears the wisdom of life we've gained and share our experiences with them, doesn't it make more sense to draw them near, keep them under our wing? Of course, every angel has to eventually crawl out from underneath our protection and fly solo. But until they're on their own, let's hold them close! Our children will always be close in our hearts, but the time we actually have them physically close is so short.

Consequence #3: Takeaway

The last consequence we're going to talk about—takeaway—is more effective for school-age children than their younger siblings. Generally speaking, younger children need to experience immediate consequences for their actions in order to develop the understanding, "When I do this, that happens." Their sense of time and their understanding of cause-and-postponed-effect are still emerging. For this reason, delayed punishment is not effective. Toddlers and preschoolers simply cannot make the connection between their inappropriate behavior and punishment that comes later.

But for older children, takeaways are a good way to positively punish. "You deliberately broke your sister's game. You may not break things. You cannot use your video game until tomorrow after school." "You were disrespectful to me. You cannot go bowling Friday night."

The tough part about the takeaway strategy is following through, since a certain amount of time will have elapsed before the actual consequence. By Friday "no bowling" night, your child is no longer exhibiting the inappropriate behavior—and you've probably mellowed a bit. At dinnertime he's likely to plead, protest, and exclaim, "It's not fair." It's kind of like resisting arrest. And you're going to be hard pressed not to give in. Don't!

What does your child want, and what does he really need?

Most adults, like children, have unlimited wants and limited needs. A few of us exhausted mothers have realized that the more you have, the more you have to take care of. There's something to be said for simplicity! But think about it. Even if you have a closet full of clothes, you usually only wear an armful of outfits on a regular basis. Of all the pots and pans under the counter, you only use a few; most of the rest hardly get touched. Look at all the stuff in your garage or storage area. Most of it is just taking up space, right?

As mothers, even we can have unlimited wants. And while most of us have learned to control our buying impulses (because of finances, space limitations, lifestyle choices, or priorities), some of us have not, which is why more than half of the families in our country live with an incredible amount of debt. It's so easy to go along with a society that says "more is better," "bigger is better," and "the best is better"!

Because of the affluence of our society and the availability of goods and services—even in remote areas, thanks to superstores (and I really do mean thanks; I love superstores)—we have learned to take all our stuff for granted. We've come to believe that our affluent lifestyles are a right and not necessarily a privilege. We've gotten used to having more clothes than we wear, homes that provide more than shelter, food that's not just for nourishment, and entertainment that's always at our fingertips. No wonder so many of us are overindulged—and in turn, overindulge our children.

Our motivation is usually good. We want the best for our children. We want them to have what we had—or what we didn't have. But regrettably, our good intentions produce outcomes that are less than beneficial. Influenced by media advertising, their peers, and our behavior as mothers, our children grow up without consumption boundaries; without an understanding of how to make purchasing decisions based on need and financial resources; and most importantly, without thankfulness and appreciation for all they have. They never learn to distinguish between a need and a want. Children see it, and they want it. If candy tastes good, then more candy should taste better. If their friends have electronic games, then they want electronic games. It's a difficult mind-set to crack.

Here's where discipline comes in. Beyond our behavior and role modeling, the best way we can help our children understand *want* versus *need* and *privilege* versus *right* is to place limits on them. By using takeaways as a socialization and guidance strategy, our children will start to experience appreciation and gratefulness.

What are takeaways?

Takeaways are things that our children want to have that we don't allow them to have, or activities they want to do that we don't allow them to do. The *want* part is key. Takeaways distinguish between want and need. Perfect little angels need warm clothes, food, rest, shelter, and love. These are needs that we should never, ever take from our children. A child shouldn't have to go out in the cold because he forgot his coat. We wouldn't keep a child from sleep, and we shouldn't withhold food or love.

Why should we avoid using food as a takeaway?

Of course, there's a difference between food for nourishment (breakfast, lunch, and dinner) and food for enjoyment or entertainment (desserts or snacks). Personally, I'm not into using any kind of food as a takeaway; I'd rather limit snacks from the start. But using a dessert or snack as a takeaway isn't the same as making a child miss a whole meal.

Sometimes when kids are acting out—and kids of all ages seem to act out around dinnertime—we're tempted to send them to their room without eating just to get them away from us. But sending children to bed without dinner is an age-old discipline strategy that I personally don't endorse. During this stressful time of the day, I think it's more effective to redirect them, use a time-out, or just send them to their room until dinner.

Children are still growing even into their twenties, and withholding meals can cause headaches, low blood sugar, dehydration—and even greater behavioral problems. We want to help our children, not hurt them.

I have to admit, though, there *are* times when children need sleep more than food. Ever send a crying, protesting preschooler to her room, only to find she is sound asleep when you check on her? Remember, one of the major reasons angels misbehave is lack of sleep.

Furthermore, there *are* times when it's appropriate to ask children to leave the table. If a child is playing with his food and refuses to eat even after subtle encouragement, he's probably not hungry. Hungry children eat. In this case, sending him away from the table is more of a logical consequence than a takeaway. "If you can't sit quietly without playing, you must leave the table." At our home the kids usually don't want to leave the table, because meals are a time of family connection and fun.

What makes takeaways so effective?

Takeaways are a powerful parenting tool. When all other mommy maneuvers fail, most children listen and respond quickly to a request that involves a takeaway as a consequence. But be careful not to use a takeaway as a threat without following through. Takeaways can be crushing and memorable, and that's why they're so effective for teaching children the consequences of their actions. We usually only have to follow through with this strategy a few times before our angels come to understand that when we suggest a takeaway, we're not joking. This is serious stuff!

The effectiveness of the takeaway strategy is based on our ability and consistency to follow through. And that's definitely the hard part. But over time, if we're consistent, just the proposition of a takeaway can be enough to stop our children's inappropriate behavior.

Recently my husband and I went shopping at our local home-improvement superstore, kids in tow. (Did I tell you I love superstores?) After visits to this store, we always like to stop at a particular fast-food restaurant, because it has an indoor playroom with an enormous climbing structure perfect for helping children burn up pent-up energy (especially in the winter in the Northeast). Well, our children must have thought they were already in the playroom, because as my husband and I were debating the merits of various bathroom cabinets, they climbed one of those ladders marked "only for trained and certified employees"; gave the baby a ride on a loading trolley; and ran laps around aisle four until a superstore employee finally returned them to us—with justified annoyance—for their own safety. We were in the wrong, of course; we were pricing cabinets, not parenting. So we gathered our children next to us and gave them strict instruction not to move. The final domino fell, however, when the older children convinced the preschooler to sit on the display potty. Thank goodness she didn't really go.

My husband and I left the store and drove right by the fast-food-and-mega-fun emporium with a car full of protesting kids crying, "We're sorry. We'll never do it again." And they haven't. The minute they start those kinds of antics in the store, they remind each other of the time Mommy and Daddy actually followed through and really drove by their favorite restaurant. If only we followed through more often!

What are some other takeaways to consider?

Takeaways should relate to the behavioral issue involved or to something the child values. Good takeaways include toys, games, extracurricular activities, after-school classes, special trips, birthday parties (not the child's own party, although I thought about it once), and family fun. Some things are off limits. For example, even though my children have referred to me as the meanest mommy in the world, I wouldn't take away their favorite stuffed animal or cuddly blanket. That's really mean. Those are comfort items. The idea is to take a privilege away, but not the child's security, self-respect, or ability to cope.

Following a parent workshop I led, a mother from the audience approached me to say she disagreed with the idea of using a birthday party as a takeaway. She thought it was too extreme and shouldn't be done. Extreme? Absolutely! That's why I use it. If my child can't behave with me at home or with his teacher in school, do I really want him misbehaving at a party at someone else's house? And more importantly, do I want my child to think that going to a birthday party is a right, just because the envelope has his name on it? A birthday party—any party—is a privilege. And as a takeaway, it's fair game. In fact, at our house, almost every activity except church and school is fair game. (Although once, in a desperate moment, I even threatened to take away Sunday school.)

Is the takeaway penalizing you or your child?

There are some activities that I *could* take away, but I don't. Why? Because following through could affect me more than the children. Taking away my children's outdoor playtime doesn't set my children up to succeed, and it could make my mothering tasks more difficult. Children, after all, are full of energy. They learn with their whole bodies. They need time to experiment with movement and work off some of that limitless liveliness. Now that doesn't mean I can't take away a specific outdoor activity, such as skating, bike riding, or basketball. The specifics are up for grabs. But having some active outdoor time is good for kids—and for moms—because it improves their health, reduces their stress, and helps them sleep better. And I'm all for that!

Watching television is another activity I don't like to use as a takeaway. I know, there are a million and one debates about children and television. What to watch? How much is too much? We don't watch a lot of TV in our home, but I rarely take all television away from my kids unless it's a last resort. Why? Because I need a last resort! Every mommy needs a you-better-believe-it, I'm-not-messing-around-now takeaway in her arsenal. For my children, a TV takeaway really works. For other children, what really works is taking away an electronic game, a CD player, or time on the computer.

With four kids and a husband who travels frequently, I have times when I need to head down to the laundry room, take a shower, or just enjoy some silence. How do I make those things happen when I'm the only parent at home? I pop in a video. Then I'm almost guaranteed thirty to sixty minutes of uninterrupted alone time. Why would I use TV as a takeaway when it helps me so much?

Let's face it. Our perfect little angels aren't going to act perfectly all the time. Sometimes they're not going to listen to us, even when we're trying our very best to guide them. That's when consequences like time-out, stay-with-me, and takeaway become such effective strategies. But whatever strategy we use, the key to success is to follow through. When we consistently follow through and do what we say we're going to do, our angels learn that staying within limits is the safest, freest, and happiest way to fly.

How can you become the kind of mother you want to be?

Earning
Your Own
Angel *Wings*

Has your perfect little angel ever had a "fit"? "Having a fit" is the phrase my grandmother likes to use for throwing a temper tantrum—that basic, irrational response children have when they don't get their way, complete with kicking, screaming, crying, and sometimes, for greater effect, lying on the floor and refusing to get up. While tantrums are irrational, they're not totally unpredictable. Most of the time, a child who has a fit is also struggling with extreme exhaustion, frustration, the inability to communicate, hunger, over stimulation, or just having too many things happening at once.

Children aren't the only ones who have fits, however. Moms have fits too—and for some of the same reasons.

The other night I couldn't get my children to understand

what I wanted them to do. I thought my directions were pretty straightforward: "Go to bed." But they all began demanding things at the same time.

"Where are my pajama bottoms?" *The top and bottom were together when I laid them out.*

"Is this too much toothpaste?" *Yes, if the toothpaste is overflowing on the floor, that's too much.*

"Could I have something to eat?" *Absolutely not. Are you crazy? You just brushed your teeth. If you had eaten your dinner, you wouldn't be hungry. Do you know how many meals and snacks I've prepared and cleaned up just today?*

And then my mind started to talk out loud. Suddenly I was spinning out of control and spurting out every good thing I had ever done for these children. I was having a fit. "I took you to the park today and we had a picnic and I colored with you and read books and did your laundry and cleaned the bathroom," I cried. "You don't appreciate anything I do!"

Of course, nothing in my tirade had anything to do with going to bed, and no one needed to hear it—especially my children. But sometimes you just say what you say. Then the tantrum began in earnest. I started storming around the house, picking up the dregs of the day: shoes here, books there, wet towels, a half-eaten bagel.

Then I threw something against the wall: two wet towels that landed in the laundry basket. I wanted to throw something that would shatter, but I figured I didn't want to break anything of my own; and besides, the only person who would be picking up the shattered mess was me. So I settled for the towels.

My children were silent and probably a bit frightened. I finally got them to bed and asleep. Then I took a long, hot shower and started to regain my sanity—and my conscience. I felt like a jerk! I was looking at my sour, wet-headed face in the bathroom mirror and feeling sorry for myself when the steam unveiled a message scrawled across the glass. It said, "I Love Mom."

And in that moment, I realized that my children really do appreciate all the things I do for them; and more than that, they love me. Well, at least the one who can write does! Being a mom isn't a self-sacrifice at all; it's who I am. It's what I do.

The Mother We Want to Be

Before our angels were born, we all dreamed about the wonderful mothers we wanted to be. But the basic framework for our parenting styles didn't come from our imagination; it came from our own experiences as children. Many of us had parents who spoke to us in ways that gave us security and comfort, even when they were reprimanding us. We want to duplicate those feelings in our own children. Others of us had parents who spoke in ways that were hurtful, engendering insecurity and fear. We don't want to duplicate *those* feelings. But we at least know what kind of mother we *don't* want to be.

Some of us remember childhoods in which our parents had great intentions, but they never seemed to follow through on their promises to be at our games and recitals, read books with us every day, and just spend time with us. Now, as mothers ourselves, we're determined to do these things with our own children. Others of us have certain negative experiences tucked in the back of our hearts—harsh words, loud voices, or worse. We're determined never to expose our children to the same things.

Until I became a mother, I couldn't even begin to understand and appreciate the lives of my parents. Now I know what they went through. And I know that much of who I am as a mom is because of them.

Remember, the basic framework of your parenting style comes from your own experiences as a child. You may want to duplicate these experiences for your own children or work hard to give them a more positive childhood.

Don't Go There

Unfortunately, the realities of everyday mothering—exhaustion, impatience, nonstop activity, financial pressure, and more—can quickly send us to parenting places we never intended to go. We say things to our children we wish we could take back. We ignore our children or lash out in anger often intended for someone else. We moralize, letting too much personal frustration show.

An occasional slip is part of being a mom. But for the most part, when we're disciplining our kids, we need to avoid such things as:

- Name calling

- Humiliation

- Shame

- Threats

- Generalizations

- Emotional outbursts

- Yelling

- Sarcasm

Of course, there's no excuse for physically hurting our children—ever. Some moms may need counseling or support to help them control their anger and impatience. If you often get angry with your child, feel like you want to hurt him, or do actually hurt him, get help. Speak with your doctor or your child's pediatrician. Talk to your pastor or religious leader, or contact your local child-services association. Asking for help doesn't mean you're a bad mom. On the contrary, asking for help means you care and want to be a better mother. We all need help sometimes.

Physical abuse is an obvious no-no. But it isn't the only kind of abuse that leaves scars. There's no truth to the childhood phrase "Sticks and stones can break my bones, but words can never hurt me." Name calling, shaming, generalizing, and other types of verbal abuse can be just as emotionally harmful to a child as physical abuse. Yes, there are going to be times when all of us fail as mothers. We're human. But it's not OK to continually humiliate or threaten our children. It doesn't teach them positive behavior. It teaches them timidity and insecurity and rage and resentment.

If you were learning something new—perhaps the rules and values of another culture—what would you want your teacher to be like? Think back to the schoolteachers of your childhood. We usually remember the best and the worst. Would you want your teacher to be harsh, demanding, and cruel, or would you want your teacher to be compassionate, encouraging, and understanding?

A mother's greatest role is that of teacher. Will we be harsh and cruel with our kids, or compassionate and understanding? Being compassionate doesn't mean being a pushover, however. The best teachers are never pushovers. Rather, as mommies we need to set loving boundaries and apply firm, consistent consequences for overstepping those boundaries. We can't be weak. Loving and teaching our children with compassion and understanding takes more fortitude and strength than yelling at them and putting them down.

Why should you encourage your child?

From the first day our children were born, they began looking to us for encouragement and support—for reassuring words, a smile, a hug, an endearing look. Our children search our faces, watch our bodies, and listen to our words to see our reactions to everything they do. They search for themselves in our responses. They look to us almost as if they are looking into a mirror.

Perfect little angels want to please, to do the right thing, to be accepted. Our encouragement or lack of encouragement shapes their self-esteem, their motivation to succeed, and their willingness to learn. Proper encouragement and guidance gives them the ability to think independently, make appropriate life decisions, and appreciate who they are and what they can become. The lack of encouragement leaves them feeling empty and disconnected. Continual criticism leaves them feeling defeated, confused, and insecure.

Your encouragement or lack of encouragement
shapes your child's self-esteem, motivation to succeed,
and willingness to learn.

Why shouldn't you call your child "bad" if she is doing bad
things?

"You're a bad girl." "You're a whiner." "You're a baby."

Ever said one of those things to your child? Perhaps you went a step further and said, "You're stupid" or "You're a pain."

Unfortunately, it has become a cultural norm to complain about others. In traffic, we exclaim about the guy in the car in front of us: "He's a jerk." We nitpick about the bagger at the grocery store: "He's so slow." We even complain about our relatives: "She's mean." Speaking negatively about others has become a habit for many of us. We do it, our children hear it, and they learn to do it too. Sometimes we even direct our negative words toward them.

We need to understand that words are powerful. We all have memories from childhood of words that parents, teachers, friends, or other children said that really hurt us. Those harsh words still hurt us today when we think of them. They're stuck in our minds forever. We don't want to hurt other people that way, do we? We especially don't want to hurt our children that way. We need to relearn so many things when we become moms!

Let's look at the example, "You're a bad girl." Maybe you're thinking, "That doesn't sound so terrible." But in saying those words, "bad girl," we're implying that the child is bad. We're telling her that *she* is the problem, when the real problem is her behavior. We're not separating the angel from the action. There's a subtle difference in wording but a profound difference in meaning between "You're bad" and "You made a bad choice." Remember, all children are perfect little angels, even though their actions at times may not be.

I don't even like the word *bad*, except in the context of bad hair days, milk gone bad, and bad as a synonym for *good*. (Are you old enough to remember those days?) The words *bad* and *angel* just don't go together. Is it inappropriate or "bad" when your child bites another child, breaks something because of reckless behavior, or talks back to you? Sure it is. But calling her "bad" probably won't help her make a good choice in the future. And that's our goal as moms: to teach our children how to make appropriate choices, even when we're not there to guide them.

Children do a lot of things that are wrong, crazy, unsuitable, and inappropriate. They make bad choices. But they're still learning— and they're still angels.

What happens when you continually call your child names or generalize about his behavior?

Imagine a child who is continually reprimanded with the words, "You're stupid." He will probably respond in one of two ways over time. The first is to develop an unhealthy desire to succeed at all costs. His goal is to prove that what the person said was wrong. And in fact, he may grow up to be a great success. In that case, was the motivation really so bad? Absolutely. Such a person will never feel any self-worth, despite his numerous accomplishments.

The second response to being constantly told, "You're stupid," is to accept and believe that characterization as fact. "She always calls me stupid. I must be stupid. Why try? I'm not capable of success." Such a person has little chance of ever feeling good about himself. And of course, children have similar responses to other names, labels, and generalizations: "You're clumsy." "You're ugly." "You're a baby." "You're a liar." "You're a bully." "You're messy."

How can you express your disapproval without name calling?

To describe your child's behavior without calling him a name, try putting the "a" back in *angel*. Instead of saying, "You're a whiner," drop the "a" and say, "You're whining." Better yet, describe the behavior so your child understands specifically what he is doing wrong: "You're talking in a squeaky, high-pitched voice, and I can't understand you." "Use your words. I can't understand you when you are crying and talking at the same time."

*To avoid calling your child a name, put the
"a" back in angel. Instead of saying, "You're a
whiner," drop the "a" and say, "You're whining."*

Should you let your child know how you're feeling? What should you do?

My work in early-childhood education has given me lots of practice when it comes to speaking and guiding children with positive words. I suppose I have had an easier transition into some aspects of motherhood because of my experience as a teacher and administrator. My husband calls me "the expert" (as in, "You do something; you're the expert," when our toddler is on the floor in the mall screaming). But it's always much easier to teach other people's children than it is to teach your own. I don't always use what I know—and I feel guilty about that.

Because of what I know, I try to never call my children names, label them, generalize about their behavior, or compare them. I even try not to think nasty thoughts about them, because I believe children have a keen sense of intuition. The emphasis is on the word *try*, because, to my deep regret, I have done all those things at one time or another.

But I'm learning. Now, instead of reverting to negative, childish reactions when I'm irritated with my children, I try to tell them how I feel: "When you push your little brother, it makes me furious." "When you cry instead of using your words, it frustrates me." "When you break my lamp after I tell you to stop throwing the ball in the house, I want to scream. It makes me so angry." Calmly telling my children that I'm upset doesn't seem to have the same self-cleansing effect as a total mommy tantrum. But then, sanely expressing my feelings doesn't come with a guilt hangover either.

Angel **Tip**

Instead of calling your child names or yelling when you are angry, tell her how you feel and why. Name your emotion.

Words are so powerful! With them, we mommies can build our children up or tear them down. Which will we choose? The only way we can become the mothers we really want to be is by learning to control our tongues. By speaking words of compassion, encouragement, and understanding to our perfect little angels, we can help them develop the courage and self-confidence to fly. And in the process, we just might earn our own set of angel wings.

How can you build on success?

Unveiling
Your Perfect
Little *Angel*

I truly believe that in every situation, in everything we do, something positive can be learned. Often the lesson is simply "I'll never do that again!" For example, you can't Armor All kitchen floors; they're shiny, but they're slippery. You can't glue on Girl Scout badges; they always fall off. And you can't use dishwashing liquid in the laundry; it always overflows. I've also learned that letting arguments go doesn't make me a loser; making mistakes and admitting them doesn't make me less smart; and being a good mother requires everyday, on-the-job training.

Ten Keys for Taking Care of Mommy

In that everyday, on-the-job learning process, I've learned that mothers need to take care of themselves. We can't care for our children the way we want to—and the way they need us to—if we're constantly tired, stressed-out, physically unfit, and always at the end of our rope.

So what can you do to take care of yourself? Here are ten keys that you can put into practice, starting today:

1. Exercise

You've heard it before, but it's really true: Nothing can take the place of exercise to lower your anxiety, raise your energy level, and give you overall better health. Take a brisk walk, head to the gym, or pop in an exercise video. Make it a priority. You can't take care of others unless you take care of yourself first.

2. Take time for you

We tend to think that good mothering means giving all your time and energy to your children. Without time for ourselves, however, we become resentful. Join a club, go shopping, or just sit down and relax.

3. Hang out with other moms

In these days of busy schedules, and with parents and siblings often living far away, it's easy to feel isolated as a mother. Why not join a moms' club or playgroup? Being around and talking with other mothers gives you the support and adult conversation you need. Plus you'll probably pick up some fresh ideas for effective parenting.

4. Make baby-sitting arrangements

In order to put these first three keys into practice, you're going to need someone to watch your children. Trade baby-sitting with a mommy friend, hire someone who is trustworthy, or ask your husband. Join organizations that offer childcare. Quite often, exercise programs, church activities, and parent-education workshops have built-in childcare arrangements.

5. Create your own support group

Surround yourself with people you can talk to about your child and mothering issues. Choose a pediatrician, preschool program, and church where you feel comfortable asking for advice.

6. Prepare a survival kit

Have a special toy or video handy for days when you just need a break. Look for sales at superstores and hide the goodies for later. Check out books, computer games, videos, and DVDs from your local library.

7. Count to ten

Before you yell at your child, flip out about a mess, or start singing the "poor mommy" song, count to ten. As a stress-reducer, it really works. (Unless your child is coloring on the wall; don't count—just grab the crayon.)

8. Take a few deep breaths

Remember those birthing classes? Lots of mothers say the instruction didn't help much with labor—but it can help with parenting. When you feel tense, breathe in deeply through your nose and exhale through your mouth. Continue until you regain your patience and self-control. (Whenever I start to do this, my kids know I'm really upset.)

9. Call a friend

When you need a break, call someone who will listen to your frustration—not necessarily someone who wants to help you solve your problems, but someone who will validate your feelings. My husband is a great problem solver; my girlfriend knows how to just listen. Sometimes an empathetic ear is all you need.

10. Picture your child asleep

This works two ways. One, thinking about that angelic face sound asleep on the pillow reminds you to count your blessings. Two, it reminds you that no matter how hard the day is, your child will eventually go to bed and fall asleep. (Granted, at 9 a.m., bedtime can seem a distant dream.)

Eight Keys for Building on Parenting Success

As we've said throughout this book, there is a perfect little angel inside every child. Our job as mommies is to find the angel and unveil him. While we've discussed many strategies for doing this, our ultimate success comes down to eight keys:

1. Praise and encourage your child.

2. Be positive.

3. Be patient.

4. Stay connected to your child.

5. Have positive conversations with your child.

6. Ask your child questions.

7. Let your child know that it's OK to make mistakes.

8. Never forget that inside your child is a perfect little angel.

Let's look at some of these keys more closely.

Praising and Encouraging Your Child

"Good job!" "Keep trying." "You can do it!"

Everyone is encouraged by words of praise and support. Think about the times your husband or someone close has said, "You're a good mom. I'm so impressed with the way you care for your children." How did that make you feel? (If no one has said that to you, wouldn't it feel nice if they did?) A real compliment can make you feel capable, confident, and motivated to continue doing a good job. On the other hand, if no one ever acknowledges your efforts, you can feel unappreciated, ignored, and less motivated to keep going.

Of course, praise and encouragement shouldn't be the only motivating factor for good behavior. Doing what's right shouldn't be based solely on recognition, rewards, and having others think well of us. Even as adults, some of us are still struggling to understand that self-worth, happiness, and contentment come from within—not from material possessions, acceptance, or praise.

Why should you praise and encourage your child, when ultimately she must learn to be self-motivated?

Our children are learning. They are learning how to behave, how to find self-worth, how to become responsible persons capable of making appropriate and positive decisions. This is no easy task. They need our encouragement to keep moving forward, to stay in the game, to believe they can succeed. Everyone needs a cheerleader, and children especially need a mommy's praise and encouragement in order for the perfect little angel within them to be manifested.

Watch an infant, and you will see her look to her mother for approval after making a cooing sound or clapping her hands. Watch a toddler come to his mother after a fall for reassurance that he will be OK. Watch a preschooler learn the alphabet as her mother points to the letters, smiles, and offers praise. Even a high-school football player will look to the stands, hoping to see the familiar faces of his parents.

Children thrive with continued encouragement and praise. Studies show that babies who are encouraged, hugged, loved, and cared for are much more likely to grow up confident and optimistic. When they're profoundly deprived of human contact and love, however, critical areas of their brains remain underdeveloped[1]. Isn't that amazing? What we as mommies say and do to our children shapes not only their attitudes but the actual formation of their brains!

Can you praise your child too much?

In almost everything in life, it's possible to have too much of a good thing. Holidays wouldn't be so special if they happened every day, ice cream wouldn't be as sweet if you ate it at every meal, and a starfish found on the beach wouldn't seem like such a treasure if hundreds of starfish were lying all over the sand. Likewise, praise can be overdone to the point that our words lose some of their impact and meaning.

But there is one thing we can never give too much of to our perfect little angels, and that's love. What's the difference between love and praise? Love is the all consuming, unconditional feeling of commitment and devotion we have for our children. Every child should know that his mother loves him unconditionally for the most basic reason: because he is her child. Praise, on the other hand, is the act of telling our children through words or actions that we are pleased with their efforts. Love is about the child; praise is about the actions of the child. Our children need to know that even though we may be upset with their behavior or displeased with their actions at times, we always love them.

Remember, love is for your child; praise is for her actions.

What's the best way to praise your child?

As moms we all have different personalities and temperaments.

Some of us are born cheerleaders; others of us have to make a conscious effort to verbally support our children.

It's like the difference between husbands and wives. We might ask our husbands, "Don't you love me? You never say it." And our husbands look at us quizzically and respond, "Of course I do. Look at all the things I do for you and the children." We want to hear the words, while they feel that their actions say much more than the words. Good mothering requires both: the actions that convey our love and support for our children, and the words that actually say, "I love you" and "I support you." One may come more naturally than the other, but both are necessary.

So what are the best ways to praise our children? Here are a few tips:

- *Be specific.* Describe what your child did: "You picked up the toys and put them on the shelf. Thank you." "You wanted that candy bar in the store, but you put it back when I asked you to. Good listening."

- *Make "you" statements instead of "I" statements.* Say, "You must feel relieved that you cleaned up your room in time to watch TV," instead of, "I am proud of you for cleaning up your room. Now you can watch TV." The use of *you* focuses the praise on the actions of the child and the consequences he experiences from his own choices, rather than on your validation of his efforts.

- *Praise success and efforts of near-success.* "You were really angry, but you didn't hit your brother. That takes control.

Good job." "You started to cry because you wanted to have another cookie. Then you stopped yourself and used your words. When you use your words, I can understand you."

Spending Time with Your Angel

I'm a frequently worried, trying-to-get-things-done, always-thinking-ahead kind of mother. Know anyone like that? (Pretty much describes the motherhood role!) Now those are great traits if we're planning an emergency management rescue plan or organizing an elaborate wedding. But they can also be overbearing and even annoying if we forget to relax, go with the flow, and enjoy spending time with our angels. As moms we really need to:

- Pay attention to safety, but relax

- Be with our children not just physically, but mentally

- Be flexible and follow our children's interests

- Enjoy the benefits of planning, but realize that things don't always go as planned

Staying Connected to Your Child

When three o'clock comes each afternoon, I head to the school, eager to pick up my children. After several hours alone getting work done, cleaning up around the house, and deciding on a dinner plan, I actually miss them. But too often, as soon as they hop in the car—whether they're tired and quiet or wired and anxious to tell me about their day—I start to think ahead. Instead of supporting their quiet transition from school to home or joining in their lively conversation about who threw up in the auditorium, the intricate rules of a new recess game, or the gross Sloppy Joes served at lunch, I'm thinking about their homework. What assignments have to be completed that evening? Or I'm thinking about my own work. What do I have to do after the kids are in bed?

I've found that I have to really concentrate on being with my children. I have to make a concerted effort to listen to them and have positive conversations with them. I have to consciously switch off my "what's next" mode and switch on the "here and now" mode. And the truth is, I enjoy hearing about a day in the life of a third grader. We have a routine; the homework will get done. But the opportunities I have to connect with my children will be lost if I don't take advantage of the times I have with them, if I don't seize the moment.

To stay connected with your child, consciously switch off your "what's next" mode of thinking and make a conscious effort to appreciate and enjoy the times you have together.

Having Positive Conversations

Children don't usually make plans to have conversations with us. We have to be physically available to them in order to stimulate conversation. If we're with them, we're bound to hear what's on their minds. But if they constantly have to seek us out or wait for our schedules to open up, if they have to contend with frequent lack of interest or diverted attention, they will eventually stop talking to us.

Children are very immediate, especially when it comes to their feelings, emotions, and worries. When your child wants to talk, do your very best to make yourself available; otherwise, the opportunity may be lost. Then, after a conversation, make sure you follow up. If your child was worried about a math test, ask her, "How did it go?" (Not, "What grade did you get?") If she mentioned once that she would like to go Rollerblading, arrange a time to skate. We can't give our children everything they want or soothe away every worry, but we can show them that we're available and we're listening.

How can you promote more positive conversations with your child?

Here are a few ideas for fostering an atmosphere that stimulates conversation:

- *Appreciate your child's unique personality.* Some children are eager to chat. Others need time to open up to conversation. Know your child, and don't push her to be something she's not.

- *Be sensitive to your child's primary needs.* If your angel is starving, headed to the bathroom, or just relaxing after a busy school day, he may not want to talk at that moment. Try to take care of his primary needs before initiating conversation.

- *Allow for conversation rituals and individual preferences.* Some children may need time to play quietly or hang out in their rooms before volunteering information and

129

answering questions. Many will save their most intimate thoughts for "tuck-in time." Even if your child no longer needs you to actually pull up the covers, lingering a bit in her room before lights-out gives her a quiet, unhurried opportunity to share her thoughts and dreams.

- *Do things together.* Riding in the car, having a snack at the kitchen table, and doing chores together are all good times for conversation. When people are doing things together, conversations spontaneously emerge; sharing seems less intimidating and more natural.

- *Set aside time for your child.* Children are more likely to initiate conversations when they sense our interest in being with them. So set aside time to spend with your angel. If you're a working mom, set a time each day when you check in with your child and chat by phone.

- *Appreciate the silence.* Just being together, mother and child, not uttering a word, is time well spent. Build a comfortable relationship with your angel by learning to enjoy each other's company in silence.

- *Ask questions.* Many children need a little prompting or gentle questioning to help them open up and share their thoughts. Try asking questions that require more than a yes or no answer. "How do you feel about . . . ?" "What would you do if . . . ?" "Help me understand. Tell me what happened."

Angel **Tip**

*If your child really wants to talk to you, stop everything and
listen. If you simply can't talk (and there are those times),
say, "What you have to say to me is very important, but I
have to go to work. I'll call you as soon as I get to the office."*

How can you ask questions and address issues in a positive way?

The first key is to be *descriptive, instead of judgmental*. Say,
"Explain to me what happened" (descriptive) instead of, "How
could you do such a crazy thing?" (judgmental). Judgmental
questions or statements can easily push children into a corner,
making them feel defensive. They may begin to rationalize,
refuse to talk, or sometimes even lie. No matter how angry we
are, we have to remember that our goal is to figure out what happened and then work together with our children to make sure it
doesn't happen again.

The second key is to be *supportive instead of authoritarian*. Say,
"What do you think you should do to make sure you get your homework assignment in on time?" (supportive) instead of, "You'll do
what I say the next time you have an assignment. That's the only
way you'll get it turned it in on time" (authoritarian). Of course, as
mothers, we *are* the authority, and sometimes we have to exert that
authority. But we also have to pick our battles. If we can involve our
children in a supportive dialogue, we have the opportunity to teach
them how to solve problems, how to learn from their mistakes, and

how to work through issues instead of giving up. The list of positive lessons to be learned through dialogue is endless.

The third key is to be *respectful instead of superior*. Say, "I always found it easier to do my homework before doing anything else, but I want to hear your ideas" (respectful) instead of, "I never had a problem finishing my homework. I always completed it as soon as I got home from school. Why can't you?" (superior). When we are mutually respectful, mothers and children become better listeners. We also foster a climate that encourages dialogue, not monologue. Kids are so great to talk with! They have such fresh and uncomplicated perspectives on the world. Unfortunately, many of our conversations, especially disciplinary ones, quickly turn into frustrating, one-sided diatribes: "I'm the mother, and I'm right. You're the child, and you're wrong."

It takes practice for mothers to have real conversations with their children, not just "mommy knows best" sermons. But by being descriptive instead of judgmental, supportive instead of authoritarian, and respectful instead of superior, we show our children that we're interested in their points of view, value their feelings, and want to understand their needs and concerns. As a result, they're more likely to want to talk to us.

How can you encourage your child to come to you with questions and concerns?

Think teachable moments, not preachable moments. When your child confides in you about something that is upsetting to you, try to talk calmly with him about what to do with the information. Let your child know it's OK to make mistakes.

Suppose, for example, your child tells you his friend smoked a cigarette. What would you do? My first instinct would be to say, "I'm going to call his mother, and if I ever catch you smoking, you'll be grounded or worse!" Of course, I always reserve the right as the adult to do what I want with the information I hear, including getting other parents and children involved. But hopefully I would hold my tongue and choose my words carefully. I definitely don't want my kids to start smoking. At the same time, the fact that my child would choose to confide in me about such a sensitive subject opens a window of communication that I wouldn't want to slam shut. And what if he was trying to tell me in an indirect way that he had smoked too?

Here's what I might say: "What did you think when he was smoking?" Then, "I don't want you to smoke. It's easy to get hooked, and I want you to be healthy. If someone offers you a cigarette, say no."

Should you be a friend to your child?

Being available to our children, listening to them, supporting them, respecting them—these are important things for us to strive for as moms. Getting our children to like us is not. Sure, it would be great if our kids always thought we were fun and cool and wonderful. But we don't gain an advantage by trying to be a friend to our children. We're not their friends. We're their mothers.

Our children will have many friends in their lifetimes, but they will only have one mom!

I once heard a story about an eight-year-old child who was asked, "What are mothers made of?" He responded, "Moms are made of fluffy clouds, angel hair, and a little dab of mean." Are we mommies really *mean*? To our children we may seem that way, because we make rules, set limits, follow through with consequences, and generally keep our perfect little angels from doing whatever they want. But that's not being mean; that's loving enough to discipline.

There's a fine line between being friendly with our children and being our children's friends. Of course we should laugh and have fun together, but the main thing we should strive for is our children's respect and the love that goes along with that type of respect. Our children need to understand that we have experience and knowledge that can help guide them as they go forward in life. Yes, we appreciate our children and respect them. We're open to learning how they want to do things. But ultimately, we're their mothers, not their friends.

When our children are little, we are there to influence and discipline them. When they are older, we hope they will seek our help and advice. That is the bond we are working to create.

Putting All the Halos in a Row

As we close this final chapter, I want to suggest some questions for you to ask yourself. They're designed to help you put all the halos we've talked about in these pages in a row—to help you focus on your child's behavior, discover patterns of inappropriate behavior, and implement simple modifications to your routine or environment that will help your perfect little angel succeed:

- What behavior do you notice in your child that concerns you? Really watch your child and listen to her. Describe the behavior that you observe. Is it really inappropriate?

- Do you see a pattern associated with the inappropriate behavior? Does it take place at the end of the day? When you are in a hurry? In crowded places? When your child is tired or hungry? When you change the routine?

- Look at your own behavior in those same types of situations. Are you being a good role model? (Role modeling is the best way to teach!)

- Are your expectations for your child appropriate?

- What is your child's temperament and personality?

- What are your individual, family, and cultural levels of tolerance and acceptance for such behavior?

As you consider these questions, I want to leave you with two things to remember: First, in every child there is a perfect little angel. Second, you don't have to be a perfect mom to discover that angel and teach him how to fly. After all, the angel is already in there. You're job is simply to unveil him, to help him be who he really is. It will take love. It will take effort. And it will take a mommy's unwavering belief that one day, this angel is going to soar.

Notes

CHAPTER TWO: *Avoiding* Angel Grabbers and Success *Zappers*

1. *American Academy of Pediatrics Guide to Your Child's Sleep*, ed. George J. Cohen MD (New York: Villard Books, 1999).

2. American School Food Service Association, "Impact of Hunger and Malnutrition on Student Achievement," *School Food Service Research Review* (Spring 1989), 17–21.

CHAPTER NINE: *Unveiling* Your Perfect Little *Angel*

1. Families and Work Institute, "Rethinking the Brain: New Insights into Early Development." *Conference Report on Brain Development in Young Children* (New Frontiers for Research, Policy and Practice, 1996).